THE TRAGEDY OF
Macbeth

EDITED BY

George Lyman Kittredge

Revised by Irving Ribner

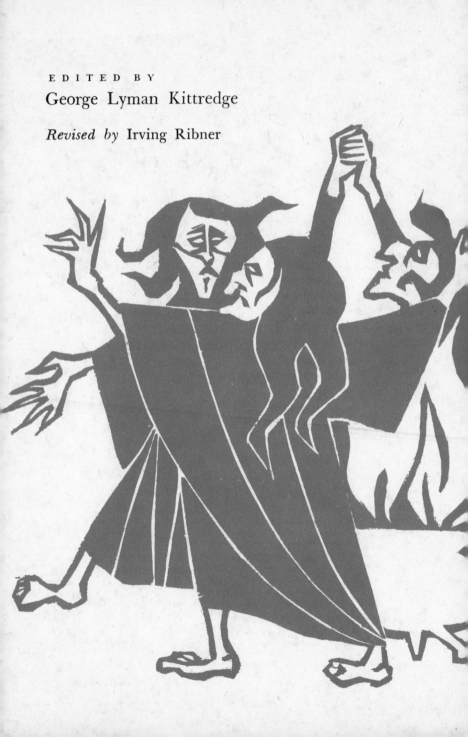

William Shakespeare

THE TRAGEDY OF

Macbeth

John Wiley & Sons, *New York* • *London* • *Sydney* • *Toronto*

ISBN 0 471 00521 5

LIBRARY OF CONGRESS CATALOG CARD NUMBER: 66-7599

PRINTED IN THE UNITED STATES OF AMERICA.

10 9 8 7 6 5 4

PREFACE

The New Kittredge Shakespeares

The publication of George Lyman Kittredge's *Complete Works of Shakespeare* in 1936 was a landmark in Shakespeare scholarship. The teacher who for almost half a century had dominated and shaped the direction of Shakespearean study in America produced what was recognized widely as the finest edition of Shakespeare up to his time. In the preface to this edition Kittredge indicated his editorial principles; these allowed a paramount authority to the Folio of 1623 and countenanced few departures from it while, at the same time, refusing to "canonize the heedless type-setters of the Elizabethan printing house." Kittredge's work was marked by a judicious conservatism and a common sense rarely found in equal measure in earlier editors of Shakespeare. In the thirty-odd years which have gone by since the appearance of this monumental volume, however, considerable advances have been made in the establishment of Shakespeare's text, and our body of knowledge about the dates, sources, and general historical background of Shakespeare's plays has vastly increased. The present revision is designed to apply this new knowledge to Kittredge's work so that it may have as much value to the student and general reader of today as it had to those of thirty years ago.

Before his death Kittredge had issued, in addition to *The Complete Works,* separate editions of sixteen of the plays, each copiously annotated. Some of the notes were unusually elaborate, but they interpreted Shakespeare's language with a fullness and precision attained by few other commentators, for Kittredge had few equals in his intimate knowledge of Elizabethan English. In freshly annotating the plays I have, accordingly, tried to use Kittredge's own notes as fully as space would permit. Where I

have repeated his distinctive language or recorded his character-
istic critical opinions, I have followed the note with the symbol
[к]; where Kittredge's definition of a term can be found in essen-
tially the same words in other editions, I have not used the
identifying symbol. Every annotator draws upon the full body
of the notes of earlier editors, and to give credit for every note
is impossible. Notes have been placed at page bottoms.

The brief introductions which Kittredge wrote for the plays
have been replaced by new ones, for what seemed like indispu-
table fact some thirty years ago often appears today to be much
more uncertain, and many new issues of which Kittredge was
not aware have been raised in recent criticism. The new introductions seek to present what are now generally agreed to be
basic facts about the plays and to give some indications of the
directions which modern criticism has taken, although specific
analyses of individual plays are avoided.

Such great authority attaches to Kittredge's text that it has
not frequently — and never lightly — been departed from. Where
changes have been made, they have usually involved the restoration of copy-text readings now generally accepted in place of the
emendations of eighteenth- and nineteenth-century editors of
which Kittredge, in spite of his extraordinary conservatism in
this regard, sometimes too easily approved. Only rarely has an
emendation been adopted in the present revision which was not
also adopted by Kittredge. All departures from the copy-texts
are indicated in the notes, emendations followed by the names
of the editors by whom they were first proposed. Wherever
Kittredge's text has been departed from for any reason, his reading is given in the notes. Modern spelling has in a few instances
been substituted for Elizabethan forms which are mere spelling
variations but which Kittredge nevertheless retained. His punc-
tuation has not been altered except in a few very rare instances.

The system of recording elisions and contractions which Kittredge explained in his introduction to *The Complete Works* has
been retained, as has his method of preserving to the fullest the
copy-text stage directions, with all additions to them enclosed
within square brackets. Although modern editors recognize the
vagueness of the place settings of Elizabethan plays and are re-

luctant to include the place designations so favoured by eighteenth- and nineteenth-century editors, much historical interest nevertheless attaches to these, and Kittredge's place designations accordingly have been retained between square brackets. Kittredge's attempt to retain the line numbering of the Globe text, which resulted in considerable irregularity in prose passages, has been abandoned, and the lines of each play have been freshly numbered. Kittredge's act and scene divisions have been retained, as has his practice of surrounding by square brackets those divisions which are not in the copy-texts.

The *New Kittredge Shakespeares* include individual editions of each of the plays, the sonnets, and the minor poems, and a new edition of *The Complete Works* in a single volume. A comprehensive introduction to Shakespeare's life, times, and theatrical milieu is available both as a separate volume and as an introduction to *The Complete Works*.

IRVING RIBNER

INTRODUCTION

The Tragedy of Macbeth

◇◇◇◇◇
◇◇◇◇◇   *Macbeth* was printed for the first time in the Folio of
◇◇◇◇◇   1623 (F¹), with act and scene divisions, but without a
Dramatis Personae. This text, upon which the present edition is
based, was set up from either a prompt-copy or a transcript of
one. The acting version it represents shows signs of having been
abridged from a longer version, possibly because of censorship
or for performance at court, the play as it stands being one of
the shortest in the entire Shakespeare canon. There are passages
in the Folio text, moreover, that are manifestly not of Shakespeare's authorship — all of III.v and IV.i.39–43 and 125–32; on
the basis of two F¹ stage directions (III.v.33 and IV.i.43), which
call for songs actually preserved in a tragicomedy by Thomas
Middleton called *The Witch,* these "Hecate scenes" have generally been attributed to Middleton, although this is by no means
certain.

DATE

That *Macbeth* was written after the accession of King James I
in 1603 is clear from allusions in the play to Banquo's descendants — among whom the King was reputed to be — and from the
very Scottish subject matter of the play. But to date *Macbeth*
more precisely is difficult, for there is no specific record of a
production earlier than April of 1611, when a performance at
the Globe was described by the astrologer Dr. Simon Forman.
There is good reason to believe, nevertheless, that *Macbeth* was
among the many plays performed at court in July and August
of 1606 for the entertainment of the king's brother-in-law, King
Christian IV of Denmark, and it may well be that our surviving

text was prepared for that specific occasion. Allusions in the play to equivocation and to the hanging of traitors have usually been taken to refer to the trial on March 28, 1606, and the hanging on May 3 of the Jesuit Henry Garnet for his complicity in the Gunpowder Plot; allusions to *Macbeth,* in turn, have been detected in various plays, such as *The Puritaine* and *The Knight of the Burning Pestle,* acted after 1606. Although none of this evidence is conclusive, that the play was composed in late 1605 or early 1606 accords with considerations of style and meter, and has generally been accepted by scholars.

SOURCES

The story of *Macbeth* represents an historical legend which through a process of telling and retelling had come by Shakespeare's time to include so much of popular folk legend and to have so suffered from deliberate distortion for immediate political purposes that truth was virtually inseparable from fiction. Shakespeare's contemporaries, in fact, made no precise distinction between historical truth and historical legend, and we have small reason to suppose that the historicity of the story as it appeared in Raphael Holinshed's *Chronicles of England, Scotland and Ireland* was at all doubted. The 1587 edition of this work was Shakespeare's immediate source.

The historical Macbeth ruled Scotland from A.D. 1040 to 1057, and from all available historical evidence, he appears to have been a good king, under whom Scotland prospered. He is called a savage tyrant in the first account of his reign in the *Chronicle* of John of Fordun, a priest who died in 1385. In the *Chronicle* of Andrew of Wyntoun, written around 1424, the story is further embellished, and we find for the first time the account of Macbeth's meeting with the Weird Sisters. In 1526 and 1527 Hector Boece printed his *Scotorum Historiae,* in which new episodes were added. To Boece's imagination we owe Banquo and Fleance, for whom there is no historical basis, and a Macduff who resembles that of Shakespeare's play rather than the Macduff of history. That Banquo should be regarded as the ancestor of the Stuart kings shows the ease with which Boece's fiction could be fused with actual history. Boece's Latin was translated into Scottish prose by John Bellenden and printed in 1536. This translation served as the basis of Holinshed's account.

In Holinshed Shakespeare found Macbeth's encounter with the Weird Sisters; the slaying of Duncan in an ambush near Inverness, engineered by Macbeth and his partisans, who resented the naming of Malcolm as Prince of Cumberland; and Macbeth's consequent seventeen-year rule as king. In this account Macbeth has some legitimate claim to the throne; whether or not he was the actual killer of Duncan is not certain, and he is reported to have ruled Scotland well for some ten years following his succession, degenerating into a tyrant only at the end, as he began to brood over the possibility that the kingdom would pass into the hands of the posterity of Banquo, who in Holinshed's version is Macbeth's accomplice in the death of Duncan. For the murder of Duncan, Shakespeare turned to an entirely unrelated account in Holinshed, the story of the murder of King Duff by Donwald. Here he found a portrait of a fearful murderer, urged on by his wife, killing his friend and guest in his own bedchamber. Here also were the prodigies that accompany Duncan's death, and most important, suggestions that were to lead to Shakespeare's conception of a murderer of such powerful imagination that he can visualize all of the elements of his crime and its consequences and be horrified by what he merely contemplates. In Holinshed's Donwald are the seeds of Shakespeare's profound psychological probing of his hero. In this account also Shakespeare found the suggestion that was to emerge as Lady Macbeth, for Donwald's wife is treated much more fully than that of Holinshed's Macbeth.

It is possible that Shakespeare drew also upon the *Rerum Scoticarum Historia* of George Buchanan, published in 1582, although no English edition of this work by the learned humanist tutor of King James appeared during Shakespeare's lifetime. Because he often read widely in preparation for his historical plays, it is not unlikely that Shakespeare consulted Buchanan's Latin treatise, although this has never really been proved. It has been suggested also that Shakespeare knew William Stewart's *Buik of the Chronicles of Scotland*, a long metrical history based upon John Bellenden. Since this remained in manuscript until the nineteenth century, it is not very likely that Shakespeare could have consulted it. A stronger case has been made for his reading of John Leslie's *De Origine, Moribus, et Rebus Gestis Scotorum,* published in Rome in 1578, but there really is little in the play that we need attribute to more than Shakespeare's sensitive reading and adaptation of Raphael Holinshed.

It has been argued — most energetically by H. N. Paul, *The Royal Play of Macbeth* (New York: Macmillan, 1950) — that Shakespeare's attention was drawn to Holinshed's account of Macbeth by an entertainment he had witnessed at Oxford in the summer of 1605. At that time one Matthew Gwinn had performed before the visiting King James his *Tres Sibyllae,* a pageant in which three sybils predicted that Banquo's descendants would rule an endless empire. There is a strong possibility that Shakespeare may have seen the pageant, for he often passed through Oxford on his way from London to Stratford, and he may have known that King James had shown pleasure at Gwinn's spectacle in praise of his mythical ancestor and that he had expressed a dislike for long plays. Macbeth deals with subject matter with which we know that the King himself was concerned, political problems, for instance, and the supernatural. James had published his own *Daemonology* in 1597, in which he had defended the existence of witches. To conclude, however, as some have done, that *Macbeth* was deliberately shaped by Shakespeare to cater to the king's interests and predilections does scant justice to Shakespeare's artistic integrity and imagination.

THE WEIRD SISTERS

Macbeth's encounter with the Weird Sisters had been a part of his legend since the time of Wyntoun's *Chronicle.* Their exact nature in Shakespeare's play, however, has been the source of considerable debate. Holinshed, following his sources, had called them "the goddesses of destiny." Kittredge has held that although they are given the form of such ordinary witches as were familiar to Elizabethan superstition, they are in fact in Shakespeare, as in earlier versions of the story, the destinies or Norns of Scandinavian mythology, neither good nor bad in themselves but the impersonal shapers of the future:

> The Norns were goddesses who shaped beforehand the life of every man. Sometimes they came in the night and stood by the cradle of the new-born child, uttering their decrees; for their office was not to prophesy only, but to determine. Sometimes they were met in wild places and at unexpected moments. Once they were seen in a remote den in the woods, weaving the visible web of doom on the day of a great battle in which many perished. Now they appear as the guardians of a favourite hero; again, they are hostile, and bent only on a man's destruction: but always and everywhere they are great and terrible powers, from whose mandate there is no appeal. In all probability, their attachment to the story goes back to the time of Macbeth himself. Their presence is due to the large infusion of Norse blood in the Scottish race, and their function is in full accord with the doctrines of Norse heathendom. That function, then, was an essential element in the history of Macbeth as it came into Shakespeare's hands. These were not ordinary witches or seeresses. They were great powers of destiny, great ministers of fate. They had determined the past; they governed the present; they not only foresaw the future, but decreed it.

If the witches are seen in these terms, the play becomes, as Kittredge indeed conceived it to be, the most fatalistic of Shakespeare's tragedies.

Still other critics have seen the Weird Sisters as ordinary Elizabethan witches, old women in communion with the Devil, who exercise their malignancy in the killing of cattle and the raising of hostile winds at sea. Some have seen them as actual demons disguised as witches. Shakespeare never really explains his Weird Sisters, but it is obvious that in the scheme of the play they can be regarded only as symbols of evil. They are deliberately shaped as contrary to nature, women with the beards of men. Their incantation is a black Mass, and the hell-broth they stir consists of the disunified parts of men and animals, creation in chaos. They wait for Macbeth and Banquo as the forces of evil wait for all men. They do not, however, suggest evil to man, and ultimately they have no control over man's acts, for the impulse to evil, in the Christian world of this play, must come from man himself. Shakespeare's witches deal in half-truths, suggesting aspects of the future that may incite the inclination to evil that is always within man because of original sin. They may, however, be resisted by the good man — as Banquo is able to resist them in spite of a temptation as great as that faced by Macbeth — for man shares in the grace of God as well as in original sin. The witches present a traditional view of evil operating through deception, posing as the friends of man, misleading him with promises of a false felicity which he pursues to his own destruction. But they do not determine, for the world of Shakespeare's play is not that of Scandinavian paganism.

THE DESTRUCTION OF MACBETH

It is thus important to recognize that Macbeth alone is responsible for the fate that befalls him. In this play Shakespeare explores the damnation of a human soul, a man of heroic proportions, with whom we can have a full measure of sympathy, who, by his own deliberate and knowing moral choice, commits a crime in violation of his own natural feelings, suffers in his isolation a hell on earth, and is finally damned. Neither the Weird Sisters nor his wife compel him to any action. Corrupted by the sin of ambition, he sets kingship above salvation. To attain the crown he knowingly embraces damnation and severs all bonds of human feeling so that he can murder his king, benefactor, kinsman, and guest in violation of the basic laws of nature. Shakespeare endows Macbeth with a power of imagination that enables him to fully perceive every aspect both of his crime and its consequences even before the act is committed, so that there is never any doubt of his own awareness of what he is doing. Unlike Othello or Lear, Macbeth never sins through ignorance; his is a total and deliberate commitment to evil.

Still, we never lose our sympathy for Macbeth; he never becomes the sinner of a cautionary moral *exemplum,* as he might have become in the hands of a lesser artist. He has a naturalness about him that makes us feel his conflicts and suffer his agonies with him. He displays upon the stage a full range of human potentiality — the greatness, the horror, and the degradation of which we all are capable. We participate in his tragedy as he reveals to us our own humanity. And in his final destruction, although there is terror, pity, and a sense of human waste, there is no feeling of negation or despair, for Shakespeare shows us a new order being reborn out of the dissolution of the old; the holy magic of King Edward the Confessor heals society in contrast to the evil of the Weird Sisters, and under Malcolm and Macduff there is hope that a new order will be reborn in Scotland.

LADY MACBETH

Macbeth's wife is one of Shakespeare's supreme creations, but we distort the play when we make her responsible for her husband's downfall. Her function is to help Macbeth destroy within himself those natural feelings that must be negated before the crime can be committed. She abets him in his crime, but she does not instigate it, and she does not force him to it; the initial suggestion is Macbeth's. To help her husband overcome his normal fears, which are symbols of his kinship to his fellow men, Lady Macbeth must deny the natural feelings within herself. Woman is normally a symbol of life and growth, and through the play her own femininity is held in contrast to the unnatural forces she would call into play. She would become unsexed, and have her milk convert to gall. She is a tragic figure herself because finally she cannot really become the unnatural creature she would make of herself. Her femininity triumphs, and her own awareness of what she has done leads to the horror of her final suffering and death.

THE COSMIC SCOPE OF THE TRAGEDY

The focus of the play is on the mind of Macbeth, and on the human plane the tragedy is worked out. But Elizabethans generally conceived of all creation as linked in a closely related system, and profound corruption on any level of it could throw all of nature out of harmony. Thus Macbeth's crime is felt not only within his little world of man but also on the level of the family, as the relation between husband and wife, which at the beginning of the play is among the closest in all literature, is slowly destroyed; at the end Macbeth can hear of his wife's death with little concern. The crime is felt on the level of the state with tyranny and rebellion in Scotland and at last an invading foreign army. It is felt in physical nature, for after Duncan's murder clouds hang over Scotland as the sun is blotted out; horses turn against man, their natural master, and finally eat one another.

Corruption on each of these levels, however, works itself out and breeds its own extinction. Macbeth's very alienation from mankind leads him to embrace death. The excesses of tyranny give rise to Malcolm's counteraction and the restoration of order in the state. Distortion and corruption in physical nature itself, symbolized by a moving forest and a man unborn of woman, lead at last to a restoration of natural order. *Macbeth* presents as powerful and all-embracing a vision of evil as has ever been portrayed in literature, but we are reminded always that evil is an unnatural and not a natural condition of humanity.

THE TRAGEDY OF
Macbeth

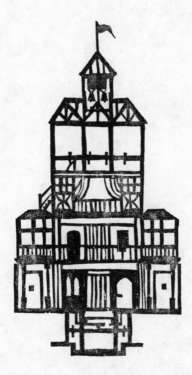

DUNCAN, *King of Scotland.*

MALCOLM,
DONALBAIN, } *his sons.*

MACBETH,
BANQUO, } *Generals of the Scottish Army.*

MACDUFF,
LENNOX,
ROSS,
MENTEITH, } *Noblemen of Scotland.*
ANGUS,
CAITHNESS,

FLEANCE, *Son to Banquo.*

SIWARD, *Earl of Northumberland, General of the English forces.*

YOUNG SIWARD, *his son.*

SEYTON, *an Officer attending on* MACBETH.

Boy, son to MACDUFF.

A Sergeant.

A Porter.

An Old Man.

An English Doctor.

A Scottish Doctor.

LADY MACBETH.

LADY MACDUFF.

A Gentlewoman, attending on LADY MACBETH.

The WEIRD SISTERS.

HECATE.

The Ghost of BANQUO.

Apparitions.

Lords, Gentlemen, Officers, Soldiers, Murderers, Messengers, Attendants.

SCENE. — *Scotland; England.*]

Act One

◇◇

SCENE I. [*Scotland. An open place.*]

Thunder and lightning. Enter three Witches.

1. WITCH. When shall we three meet again
   In thunder, lightning, or in rain?

2. WITCH. When the hurlyburly's done,
   When the battle's lost and won.

3. WITCH. That will be ere the set of sun.   5

1. WITCH. Where the place?

2. WITCH.   Upon the heath.

3. WITCH. There to meet with Macbeth.

1. WITCH. I come, Graymalkin!

2. WITCH. Paddock calls.

3. WITCH.   Anon!

ALL.   Fair is foul, and foul is fair.   10
         Hover through the fog and filthy air.   *Exeunt.*

I.I. 1–2 *When . . . rain* when shall we meet again in a storm? Witches and
demons were supposed to be particularly active in boisterous weather, which, indeed, was often thought to be caused by their spells [K].   3 *hurlyburly* tumult
or commotion, the battle described in the next scene.   8 *Graymalkin* gray cat.
The Weird Sisters are summoned by their "familiars" (attendant spirits) who have
been instructed to call when the time comes for their mistresses to depart, each
on her own evil errand. One of these demons has the shape of a gray cat, another
that of a paddock or toad [K].   9–10 2. *Witch . . . fair* SINGER; one line spoken
by "All" in F¹.

1

◈◈◈◈◈◈◈◈◈◈◈◈◈◈◈

SCENE II. [*A camp near Forres.*]

Alarum within. Enter King [Duncan], Malcolm, Donalbain, Lennox, *with* Attendants, *meeting a bleeding*
Sergeant.

KING.   What bloody man is that? He can report,
As seemeth by his plight, of the revolt
The newest state.

MAL.   This is the sergeant
Who like a good and hardy soldier fought
'Gainst my captivity. Hail, brave friend!   5
Say to the King the knowledge of the broil
As thou didst leave it.

SERG.   Doubtful it stood,
As two spent swimmers that do cling together
And choke their art. The merciless Macdonwald
(Worthy to be a rebel, for to that   10
The multiplying villainies of nature
Do swarm upon him) from the Western Isles
Of kerns and gallowglasses is supplied;
And Fortune, on his damned quarrel smiling,
Show'd like a rebel's whore. But all's too weak;   15
For brave Macbeth (well he deserves that name),
Disdaining Fortune, with his brandish'd steel,
Which smok'd with bloody execution

I.II. 3 *sergeant* an officer of much higher rank than a modern sergeant. The Folio calls him a "Captaine" in the stage direction. He may best be described, somewhat vaguely, as an officer of the guard [K].   5 *'Gainst my captivity* to prevent my being captured.   8 *spent* exhausted.   9 *choke their art* hamper each other's movements so that neither can make use of his skill as a swimmer [K].   10 *to that* as if for the very purpose (of making him a perfect rebel) [K].   12 *Western Isles* the Hebrides.   13 *kerns* Irish freebooters (not regular troops) who fought on foot. *gallowglasses* Irish soldiers who fought with axes, usually on horseback (F²; F¹: "Gallowgrosses").   14 *quarrel* HANMER; F¹: "quarry."   15 *Show'd . . . whore* appeared to have taken Macdonwald as her lover; seemed to have granted him her favour. Fortune is often regarded as a harlot, because she shows favour to all men and is constant to none [K].   19 *minion* darling, favourite.   21-2 *Which . . .*

	(Like valour's minion), carv'd out his passage	
	Till he fac'd the slave;	20
	Which ne'er shook hands nor bade farewell to him	
	Till he unseam'd him from the nave to th' chops	
	And fix'd his head upon our battlements.	

KING.   O valiant cousin! worthy gentleman!

SERG.   As whence the sun gins his reflection   25
Shipwracking storms and direful thunders break,
So from that spring whence comfort seem'd to come
Discomfort swells. Mark, King of Scotland, mark.
No sooner justice had, with valour arm'd,
Compell'd these skipping kerns to trust their heels   30
But the Norweyan lord, surveying vantage,
With furbish'd arms and new supplies of men,
Began a fresh assault.

KING.   Dismay'd not this
Our captains, Macbeth and Banquo?

SERG.   Yes,
As sparrows eagles, or the hare the lion.   35
If I say sooth, I must report they were
As cannons overcharg'd with double cracks, so they
Doubly redoubled strokes upon the foe.
Except they meant to bathe in reeking wounds,
Or memorize another Golgotha,   40
I cannot tell —
But I am faint; my gashes cry for help.

---

chops who was not able to part with Macbeth (to get rid of him) until Macbeth had ripped him up from the navel to the jaws. The form of expression is intentionally grotesque [K]. *Which* Macdonwald, although some editors have suggested Fortune or Macbeth. *chops* F¹; K: "chaps." 24 *cousin* According to Holinshed, Malcolm II had two daughters; and Duncan was the son of the elder, Macbeth of the younger. This is the genealogy adopted by Shakespeare. In fact, however, Macbeth was not so nearly related to Duncan [K]. *worthy* noble. 25 *whence . . . reflection* from where the sun first rises — the east. 26 *thunders break* POPE; F¹: "Thunders"; F²: "thunders breaking." 27 *spring* source. 31 *surveying vantage* noting an opportune moment for attack [K]. 36 *sooth* truth. 37 *overcharg'd* loaded. *double cracks* extra heavy charges of explosive, two cannon balls. 39 *Except* unless. *reeking* steaming. 40 *memorize . . . Golgotha* make the place memorable as a second Golgotha, or field of the dead. [K].

KING.	So well thy words become thee as thy wounds;
	They smack of honour both. Go get him surgeons.

[Exit Sergeant, attended.]

Enter Ross.

Who comes here?

MAL.	The worthy Thane of Ross.	45

| LEN. | What a haste looks through his eyes! So should he look |
| | That seems to speak things strange. |

| ROSS. | God save the King! |

| KING. | Whence cam'st thou, worthy thane? |

ROSS.	From Fife, great King,
	Where the Norweyan banners flout the sky
	And fan our people cold. Norway himself, 50
	With terrible numbers,
	Assisted by that most disloyal traitor
	The Thane of Cawdor, began a dismal conflict,
	Till that Bellona's bridegroom, lapp'd in proof,
	Confronted him with self-comparisons, 55
	Point against point, rebellious arm 'gainst arm,
	Curbing his lavish spirit; and to conclude,
	The victory fell on us.

| KING. | Great happiness! |

| ROSS. | That now |
| | Sweno, the Norways' king, craves composition; |

43 *become thee* Duncan sees nothing unbecoming in the Sergeant's language, nor did the Elizabethan audience. He uses the style then conventionally expected of the typical soldier — a mixture of bombast and homeliness [K]. 45 *Thane* an old Scottish title, roughly equal to "earl." 49–50 *flout . . . cold* the Norwegian banners are still flying proudly and insulting ("flouting") the Scottish sky, as they did at the beginning of the fight, but now they serve merely to cool off our soldiers, heated by the victorious battle [K]. 53 *dismal* ominous. 54 *Bellona's bridegroom* So splendid a fighter is Macbeth that Ross speaks of Bellona, the goddess of war, as taking him for her husband [K]. *lapp'd in proof* wearing well-tested armour. 55 *Confronted . . . comparisons* met him face to face and encountered each of his movements with one that matched it [K]. 57 *lavish* overconfident. 59 *craves composition* asks for terms of peace. 61 *Saint Colme's Inch* St. Columba's Island, Inchcolm in the Firth of Forth, near Edin-

	Nor would we deign him burial of his men	60
	Till he disbursed, at Saint Colme's Inch,	
	Ten thousand dollars to our general use.	
KING.	No more that Thane of Cawdor shall deceive	
	Our bosom interest. Go pronounce his present death	
	And with his former title greet Macbeth.	65
ROSS.	I'll see it done.	
DUN.	What he hath lost noble Macbeth hath won. *Exeunt.*	

◇◇◇◇◇◇◇◇◇◇◇◇◇◇◇◇◇

SCENE III. [*A blasted heath.*]

Thunder. Enter the three Witches.

1. WITCH. Where hast thou been, sister?

2. WITCH. Killing swine.

3. WITCH. Sister, where thou?

1. WITCH. A sailor's wife had chestnuts in her lap
    And mounch'd and mounch'd and mounch'd. "Give
        me," quoth I.   5
    "Aroint thee, witch!" the rump-fed ronyon cries.
    Her husband's to Aleppo gone, master o' th' Tiger;
    But in a sieve I'll thither sail
    And, like a rat without a tail,

---

burgh.   62 *dollars* Spanish dollars and German thalers were well known to the
Elizabethans. The anachronism of mentioning them in the time of Macbeth (the
eleventh century) need not worry us [K].   63–4 *deceive . . . interest* play me false
in my most important and confidential concerns [K].   *present* instant.

I.III. 2 *swine* Witches were thought to show their malice by causing the death
of domestic animals, usually by disease. Swine were often the victims, not because
witches had any special enmity for them, but merely because they were a common
possession, even of the poorest [K].   6 *Aroint thee* begone.   *rump-fed* The term
has been variously explained: (a) fed on garbage (b) fat-rumped (c) pampered.
ronyon literally, scab; scabby person; but usually (as here) a mere term of abuse
or contempt [K].   8 *in a sieve* It was believed that witches could use sieves as
boats [K].   9 *like* in the shape of.   *without a tail* When witches took the shapes
of animals, these usually had some unnatural defect.

I'll do, I'll do, and I'll do.   10

2. WITCH. I'll give thee a wind.

1. WITCH. Th' art kind.

3. WITCH. And I another.

1. WITCH. I myself have all the other,
    And the very ports they blow,   15
    All the quarters that they know
    I' th' shipman's card.
    I will drain him dry as hay.
    Sleep shall neither night nor day
    Hang upon his penthouse lid.   20
    He shall live a man forbid.
    Weary sev'nights, nine times nine,
    Shall he dwindle, peak, and pine.
    Though his bark cannot be lost,
    Yet it shall be tempest-tost.   25
    Look what I have.

2. WITCH. Show me! show me!

1. WITCH. Here I have a pilot's thumb,
    Wrack'd as homeward he did come.   *Drum within.*

3. WITCH. A drum, a drum!   30
    Macbeth doth come.

ALL.   The Weird Sisters, hand in hand,
         Posters of the sea and land,
         Thus do go about, about,
         Thrice to thine, and thrice to mine,   35
         And thrice again, to make up nine.

---

10 *do* keep the Tiger off her course by raising storms. Witches were believed to
control weather.   15 *ports they blow* the harbours to which they blow. She
controls the directions of the various winds and so can keep the Tiger away from
any port [K].   17 *card* compass.   18 *drain . . . hay* keep him at sea till all the
water on board shall be exhausted and he shall be parched with thirst [K].
20 *penthouse lid* eyelid.   21 *forbid* under a spell.   24 *cannot be lost* since
fate has decreed that it shall come safe to harbour at last [K].   28 *thumb* Frag-
ments of dead bodies were used in evil magic, and were thought to be especially
powerful if the person had died a violent death [K].   32 *Weird* (F¹: "weyward").
33 *Posters . . . land* travellers who ride through the air, posthaste, over sea and
land [K].   35 *Thrice . . . mine* three times round (hand-in-hand in the magic
dance) for thy turn, and three times for my turn [K].   37 *wound up* completed.
39 *Forres* a town south of Moray Firth, between Elgin and Nairn.   43 *question*

Peace! The charm's wound up.

Enter Macbeth *and* Banquo.

MACB.   So foul and fair a day I have not seen.

BAN.   How far is't call'd to Forres? What are these,
So wither'd, and so wild in their attire,   40
That look not like th' inhabitants o' the earth,
And yet are on't? Live you? or are you aught
That man may question? You seem to understand me,
By each at once her choppy finger laying
Upon her skinny lips. You should be women,   45
And yet your beards forbid me to interpret
That you are so.

MACB.   Speak, if you can. What are you?

1. WITCH. All hail, Macbeth! Hail to thee, Thane of Glamis!

2. WITCH. All hail, Macbeth! Hail to thee, Thane of Cawdor!

3. WITCH. All hail, Macbeth, that shalt be King hereafter!   50

BAN.   Good sir, why do you start and seem to fear
Things that do sound so fair? I' th' name of truth,
Are ye fantastical, or that indeed
Which outwardly ye show? My noble partner
You greet with present grace and great prediction   55
Of noble having and of royal hope,
That he seems rapt withal. To me you speak not.
If you can look into the seeds of time
And say which grain will grow and which will not,
Speak then to me, who neither beg nor fear   60
Your favours nor your hate.

---

hold conversation with.   44 *choppy* chapped.   45 *should be women* ought, by your
general appearance, to be women.   46 *beards* Witches were often thought to be
bearded, and indeed, the haggard old women who passed for witches must often
have had some beard [K].   53 *fantastical* imaginary, creatures of a warped imagination.   54 *show* seem, appear to be.   55–6 *with . . . hope* with present honour of
noble possession (the two thaneships) and great prediction of royal hope (the
crown). Banquo emphasizes the distinction between the mere greeting of the First
and Second Sisters, on the one hand, and the actual prediction of the Third Sister,
on the other [K].   57 *rapt* POPE; F¹: "wrapt."   57 *That . . . withal* so that he
seems carried out of himself (as in a trance) by it (your salutation) [K].   58 *seeds*
Future events are contained (in embryo) in time's seeds; their occurrence, if they
come to pass, will be the sprouting of the seeds [K].   60–1 *neither beg . . . hate*
neither beg your favours nor fear your hate [K].

1. WITCH. Hail!

2. WITCH. Hail!

3. WITCH. Hail!

1. WITCH. Lesser than Macbeth, and greater.   65

2. WITCH. Not so happy, yet much happier.

3. WITCH. Thou shalt get kings, though thou be none.
So all hail, Macbeth and Banquo!

1. WITCH. Banquo and Macbeth, all hail!

MACB.   Stay, you imperfect speakers, tell me more!   70
By Sinel's death I know I am Thane of Glamis;
But how of Cawdor? The Thane of Cawdor lives,
A prosperous gentleman; and to be King
Stands not within the prospect of belief,
No more than to be Cawdor. Say from whence   75
You owe this strange intelligence, or why
Upon this blasted heath you stop our way
With such prophetic greeting. Speak, I charge you.

Witches *vanish.*

BAN.   The earth hath bubbles, as the water has,
And these are of them. Whither are they vanish'd?   80

MACB.   Into the air, and what seem'd corporal melted
As breath into the wind. Would they had stay'd!

BAN.   Were such things here as we do speak about?
Or have we eaten on the insane root
That takes the reason prisoner?   85

67 *get* beget.   73 *prosperous gentleman* Macbeth, who has been absent from
court on an arduous campaign, knows nothing of Cawdor's treason. Banquo is
similarly uninformed. It is clear that the "assistance" given by Cawdor (I.II.52)
was secret and that Cawdor was not present in the battle. His treason had been
discovered after Macbeth left the court, and he was under arrest when the battle
took place [K].   74 *prospect of belief* farthest look into the future that belief can
take [K].   75–6 *from whence . . . intelligence* from what source you derive (owe)
this strange (supernatural) information.   81 *corporal* corporeal, of bodily substance.   84 *insane root* herb causing madness, probably hemlock or henbane.
90 *reads* considers.   92–3 *His wonders . . . his* the wonder he feels (which tends

MACB.   Your children shall be kings.

BAN.   You shall be King.

MACB.   And Thane of Cawdor too. Went it not so?

BAN.   To th' selfsame tune and words. Who's here?

Enter Ross *and* Angus.

ROSS.   The King hath happily receiv'd, Macbeth,
        The news of thy success; and when he reads   90
        Thy personal venture in the rebels' fight,
        His wonders and his praises do contend
        Which should be thine or his. Silenc'd with that,
        In viewing o'er the rest o' th' selfsame day,
        He finds thee in the stout Norweyan ranks,   95
        Nothing afeard of what thyself didst make,
        Strange images of death. As thick as tale
        Came post with post, and every one did bear
        Thy praises in his kingdom's great defence
        And pour'd them down before him.   100

ANG.   We are sent
        To give thee from our royal master thanks;
        Only to herald thee into his sight,
        Not pay thee.

ROSS.   And for an earnest of a greater honour,
        He bade me, from him, call thee Thane of Cawdor; 105
        In which addition, hail, most worthy Thane!
        For it is thine.

BAN.   What, can the devil speak true?

to make him speechless — dumb with admiration) vies with the wish he has to
utter thy praises. If the wonder remains his (if he continues to feel it to its full
extent), he will be unable to speak, and therefore the praises (being unuttered)
will not be thine [K]. *with that* by the contest between dumb wonder and the
wish to utter praise [K].   97 *Strange images of death* death in strange and dreadful forms [K].   *thick as tale* as fast as they can be counted.   98 *Came* MALONE;
F¹: "can."   *post with post* one messenger riding post after another [K].   104
earnest a small payment in advance to bind a bargain; hence, a specimen and
assurance of what is to come [K].   106 *addition* title.

MACB.   The Thane of Cawdor lives. Why do you dress me
         In borrowed robes?

ANG.   Who was the Thane lives yet,
         But under heavy judgment bears that life   110
         Which he deserves to lose. Whether he was combin'd
         With those of Norway, or did line the rebel
         With hidden help and vantage, or that with both
         He labour'd in his country's wrack, I know not;
         But treasons capital, confess'd and prov'd,   115
         Have overthrown him.

MACB.   [*aside*]   Glamis, and Thane of Cawdor!
         The greatest is behind. — [*To* Ross *and* Angus.]
             Thanks for your pains.
         [*Aside to* Banquo] Do you not hope your children shall
             be kings,
         When those that gave the Thane of Cawdor to me
         Promis'd no less to them?

BAN.   [*aside to* Macbeth]   That, trusted home,   120
         Might yet enkindle you unto the crown,
         Besides the Thane of Cawdor. But 'tis strange!
         And oftentimes, to win us to our harm,
         The instruments of darkness tell us truths,
         Win us with honest trifles, to betray's   125
         In deepest consequence. —
         Cousins, a word, I pray you.

MACB.   [*aside*] Two truths are told,
         As happy prologues to the swelling act
         Of the imperial theme. — I thank you, gentlemen. —

---

111 *combin'd* secretly allied.   112 *line* support.   113 *vantage* assistance.   *both*
Macdonwald and the King of Norway.   115 *capital* deserving of death.   117 *is
behind* remains, to follow in due succession [K].   120 *home* to the full; to its
logical conclusion [K].   121 *enkindle you unto* fire you with hope for (not, en-
courage you to try to win) [K].   125–6 *betray's . . . consequence* disappoint our
hope in something of great importance that was to follow [K].   128 *swelling act*
stately drama.   130 *soliciting* attempt to influence.   132 *earnest of success* an
assurance or pledge of what is to follow (that is, of the promised kingship) [K].
135 *image* Macbeth has a visualizing imagination. What to most men would be
a vague idea, is to him a thing seen in all the colours of reality [K].   136 *seated*

[*Aside*] This supernatural soliciting   130
Cannot be ill; cannot be good. If ill,
Why hath it given me earnest of success,
Commencing in a truth? I am Thane of Cawdor.
If good, why do I yield to that suggestion
Whose horrid image doth unfix my hair   135
And make my seated heart knock at my ribs
Against the use of nature? Present fears
Are less than horrible imaginings.
My thought, whose murder yet is but fantastical,
Shakes so my single state of man that function   140
Is smother'd in surmise and nothing is
But what is not.

BAN.   Look how our partner's rapt.

MACB.   [*aside*] If chance will have me King. Why, chance may
              crown me,
Without my stir.

BAN.   New honours come upon him,
Like our strange garments, cleave not to their mould   145
But with the aid of use.

MACB.   [*aside*] Come what come may,
Time and the hour runs through the roughest day.

BAN.   Worthy Macbeth, we stay upon your leisure.

MACB.   Give me your favour. My dull brain was wrought
With things forgotten. Kind gentlemen, your pains   150
Are regist'red where every day I turn
The leaf to read them. Let us toward the King.

---

firm and intrepid; not easily agitated [K].   137 *Against . . . nature* contrary to
my ordinary way of feeling (since I am not accustomed to fear). *Present fears*
actual objects of fear; frightful things that are before one's eyes [K].   139 *fantastical* merely imagined.   140 *single state of man* weak (unaided) human condition.
140–1 *function . . . surmise* normal senses and power of action are choked by
imagination.   141–2 *nothing . . . not* the difference between illusion and reality is
obscured.   145 *cleave . . . mould* do not fit or adapt themselves comfortably to
the wearer's form [K].   146 *use* habit, custom.   147 *Time . . . day* Time,
advancing steadily hour by hour, brings even the roughest day to an end [K].
149 *favour* pardon. *wrought* disturbed.   151 *regist'red* in my memory.

> [*Aside to Banquo*] Think upon what hath chanc'd; and,
>   at more time,
> The interim having weigh'd it, let us speak
> Our free hearts each to other.

BAN.   [*aside to* Macbeth]   Very gladly.   155

MACB.   [*aside to* Banquo] Till then, enough. — Come, friends.

>   *Exeunt.*

◊◊◊◊◊◊◊◊◊◊◊◊◊◊◊◊◊

SCENE IV. [*Forres. The Palace.*]

Flourish. Enter King [Duncan], Lennox, Malcolm,
    Donalbain, *and* Attendants.

KING.   Is execution done on Cawdor? Are not
> Those in commission yet return'd?

MAL.   My liege,
> They are not yet come back. But I have spoke
> With one that saw him die; who did report
> That very frankly he confess'd his treasons,   5
> Implor'd your Highness' pardon, and set forth
> A deep repentance. Nothing in his life
> Became him like the leaving it. He died
> As one that had been studied in his death
> To throw away the dearest thing he ow'd   10
> As 'twere a careless trifle.

KING.   There's no art
> To find the mind's construction in the face.
> He was a gentleman on whom I built
> An absolute trust.

---

153 *at more time* when we have more leisure [K].   154 *The interim . . . it* when
we have considered it in the meantime.   155 *free hearts* thoughts and feelings freely.
    I.IV. 1 *Are* F²; F¹: "or."   2 *in commission* appointed to attend to the trial and
execution of Cawdor.   9–11 *had been . . . trifle* had learned the lesson how, at
death, to part with his dearest possession (life) easily [K]. *ow'd* owned. *careless*
worthless.   12 *construction* interpretation, meaning [K].   19–20 *That the propor-*
tion . . . mine that the larger debt of gratitude (proportion) might have been on
my side of the balance; that I had paid even more than I owe.   23 *pays itself*

Enter Macbeth, Banquo, Ross, *and* Angus.

         O worthiest cousin,
The sin of my ingratitude even now   15
Was heavy on me! Thou art so far before
That swiftest wing of recompense is slow
To overtake thee. Would thou hadst less deserv'd,
That the proportion both of thanks and payment
Might have been mine! Only I have left to say,   20
More is thy due than more than all can pay.

MACB. The service and the loyalty I owe,
In doing it pays itself. Your Highness' part
Is to receive our duties; and our duties
Are to your throne and state children and servants, 25
Which do but what they should by doing everything
Safe toward your love and honour.

KING.   Welcome hither.
I have begun to plant thee and will labour
To make thee full of growing. Noble Banquo,
That hast no less deserv'd, nor must be known   30
No less to have done so, let me infold thee
And hold thee to my heart.

BAN.   There if I grow,
The harvest is your own.

KING.   My plenteous joys,
Wanton in fulness, seek to hide themselves
In drops of sorrow. Sons, kinsmen, thanes,   35
And you whose places are the nearest, know
We will establish our estate upon
Our eldest, Malcolm, whom we name hereafter

---

is its own recompense. 24–5 *our duties . . . servants* we owe you duty as a king in the same degree that children owe duty to their parents or servants to their masters; like them we can do no more than we owe, no matter how much we do. 26–7 *everything . . . honour* everything that tends to safeguard and fulfill our obligation to love and honour you [K]. 34 *Wanton* perverse, contrary, since tears are the natural expression rather of sorrow than of joy [K]. 37–8 *establish . . . Malcolm* settle the royal rank upon Malcolm as my recognized successor [K].

The Prince of Cumberland; which honour must
Not unaccompanied invest him only,   40
But signs of nobleness, like stars, shall shine
On all deservers. From hence to Inverness,
And bind us further to you.

MACB. The rest is labour, which is not us'd for you!
I'll be myself the harbinger, and make joyful   45
The hearing of my wife with your approach;
So, humbly take my leave.

KING.   My worthy Cawdor!

MACB. [*aside*] The Prince of Cumberland! That is a step
On which I must fall down, or else o'erleap,
For in my way it lies. Stars, hide your fires!   50
Let not light see my black and deep desires.
The eye wink at the hand; yet let that be,
Which the eye fears, when it is done, to see. *Exit.*

KING. True, worthy Banquo: he is full so valiant,
And in his commendations I am fed;   55
It is a banquet to me. Let's after him,
Whose care is gone before to bid us welcome.
It is a peerless kinsman. *Flourish. Exeunt.*

❖❖❖❖❖❖❖❖❖❖❖❖❖❖

SCENE V. [*Inverness. Macbeth's Castle.*]

Enter Macbeth's Wife, *alone, with a letter.*

LADY. [*reads*] "They met me in the day of success; and I have
learn'd by the perfect'st report they have more in them

---

39 *Prince of Cumberland* The throne of Scotland was elective within the
limits of the royal family. When Duncan died, the electors were not unlikely
to prefer Macbeth, Duncan's cousin, to a young and inexperienced prince
like Malcolm. But Duncan's expressed purpose of making Malcolm Prince of
Cumberland would, if it were carried out, involve his recognition as heir apparent
by the nobility, and they would thus pledge themselves to elect him when his
father should die [K]. 43 *bind . . . you* oblige me still further by receiving me
as a guest [K]. 44 *The rest . . . you* even repose, when not used in your service,
ceases to be rest and becomes toil [K]. 45 *harbinger* an officer sent ahead (when
a king intends to visit a place) to arrange proper lodgings ("harbourage") for him

than mortal knowledge. When I burn'd in desire to
question them further, they made themselves air, into
which they vanish'd. Whiles I stood rapt in the wonder   5
of it, came missives from the King, who all-hail'd me
Thane of Cawdor, by which title, before, these Weird
Sisters saluted me, and referr'd me to the coming on of
time with 'Hail, King that shalt be!' This have I
thought good to deliver thee, my dearest partner of   10
greatness, that thou mightst not lose the dues of rejoicing
by being ignorant of what greatness is promis'd thee.
Lay it to thy heart, and farewell."

Glamis thou art, and Cawdor, and shalt be
What thou art promis'd. Yet do I fear thy nature.   15
It is too full o' th' milk of human kindness
To catch the nearest way. Thou wouldst be great;
Art not without ambition, but without
The illness should attend it. What thou wouldst
      highly,
That wouldst thou holily; wouldst not play false,   20
And yet wouldst wrongly win. Thou'ldst have, great
      Glamis,
That which cries "Thus thou must do," if thou have it;
And that which rather thou dost fear to do
Than wishest should be undone. Hie thee hither,
That I may pour my spirits in thine ear   25
And chastise with the valour of my tongue
All that impedes thee from the golden round
Which fate and metaphysical aid doth seem
To have thee crown'd withal.

___

and his suite [K].   52 *wink at the hand* not see what the hand commits.
    I.v. 1 *success* in battle.   6 *missives* messengers.   7 *Weird* (F¹: "weyward").
10 *deliver* report to.   16 *milk* often used metaphorically for the kindly and gentle
qualities of human nature [K].   19 *illness* the evil quality (ruthlessness) which
should always accompany ambition [K].   21 *wouldst wrongly win* you are like a
gambler who is unwilling to cheat, and yet eager to win a stake that cannot be
won without false play [K].   24 *Hie* hasten (F⁴; F¹: "High").   25 *spirits* resolution
and energy of will.   27 *golden round* crown.   28 *metaphysical* supernatural.
28-9 *seem . . . withal* seem to intend to cause thee to be crowned with [K].

Enter Messenger.

What is your tidings?

MESS.   The King comes here to-night.

LADY.   Thou'rt mad to say it!   30
Is not thy master with him? who, were't so,
Would have inform'd for preparation.

MESS.   So please you, it is true. Our Thane is coming.
One of my fellows had the speed of him,
Who, almost dead for breath, had scarcely more   35
Than would make up his message.

LADY.   Give him tending;
He brings great news.   *Exit* Messenger.
                          The raven himself is hoarse
That croaks the fatal entrance of Duncan
Under my battlements. Come, you spirits
That tend on mortal thoughts, unsex me here,   40
And fill me, from the crown to the toe, top-full
Of direst cruelty!Make thick my blood;
Stop up th' access and passage to remorse,
That no compunctious visitings of nature
Shake my fell purpose nor keep peace between   45
Th' effect and it! Come to my woman's breasts
And take my milk for gall, you murd'ring ministers,
Wherever in your sightless substances
You wait on nature's mischief! Come, thick night,
And pall thee in the dunnest smoke of hell,   50
That my keen knife see not the wound it makes,

32 *inform'd for preparation* sent word so that I might prepare.   34 *had
the speed of* outstripped.   36 *tending* attention.   38 *fatal* (a) directed by
fate (b) deadly to Duncan.   39 *you spirits* A direct invocation to those evil
spirits, whatever they may be, that are always ready to foster murderous
thoughts [K].   40 *mortal* deadly.   42 *Make thick my blood* Blood thickened
by melancholy was thought to cause gloomy ferocity of disposition [K].   43 *remorse* pity.   44 *compunctious . . . nature* natural instincts of compassion.   45
fell cruel.   45–6 *keep peace . . . it* come between my cruel purpose and its fulfillment ("effect"), so as to prevent that fulfillment and thus to keep the peace [K].
46 *it* F³; F¹: "hit."   47 *for* in exchange for.   48 *sightless* invisible.   49 *wait*

Nor heaven peep through the blanket of the dark
To cry "Hold, hold!"

Enter Macbeth.

Great Glamis! worthy Cawdor!
Greater than both, by the all-hail hereafter!
Thy letters have transported me beyond   55
This ignorant present, and I feel now
The future in the instant.

MACB.   My dearest love,
Duncan comes here to-night.

LADY.   And when goes hence?

MACB.   To-morrow, as he purposes.
LADY.   O, never

Shall sun that morrow see!   60
Your face, my Thane, is as a book where men
May read strange matters. To beguile the time,
Look like the time; bear welcome in your eye,
Your hand, your tongue; look like the innocent flower,
But be the serpent under't. He that's coming   65
Must be provided for; and you shall put
This night's great business into my dispatch,
Which shall to all our nights and days to come
Give solely sovereign sway and masterdom.

MACB.   We will speak further.

LADY.   Only look up clear.   70
To alter favour ever is to fear.
Leave all the rest to me.   *Exeunt.*

---

on . . . mischief are on the watch to help forward any of the evil deeds to which
our nature is prone [K].   50 *pall* enshroud. *dunnest* darkest.   55 *transported
me* swept me forward as in a vision [K]   56 *ignorant* because the substantial fulfillment of one's hopes and fears is known only to the future [K]   57 *instant* present.
62 *beguile the time* deceive all observers.   67 *dispatch* management.   70 *clear*
with an unruffled countenance [K].   71 *To alter . . . fear* When a person shows
a disturbed countenance, it is always inferred that he has something on his mind
—and that may rouse suspicion among our guests [K]. *favour* countenance,
expression.

◆◇◆◇◆◇◆◇◆◇◆◇◆◇◆◇

SCENE VI. [*Inverness. Before* Macbeth's *Castle.*]

Hautboys and torches. Enter King [Duncan], Malcolm,
  Donalbain, Banquo, Lennox, Macduff, Ross, Angus,
  and Attendants.

KING.   This castle hath a pleasant seat. The air
Nimbly and sweetly recommends itself
Unto our gentle senses.

BAN.   This guest of summer,
The temple-haunting martlet, does approve
By his lov'd mansionry that the heaven's breath   5
Smells wooingly here. No jutty, frieze,
Buttress, nor coign of vantage, but this bird
Hath made his pendent bed and procreant cradle.
Where they most breed and haunt, I have observ'd
The air is delicate.

Enter Lady [Macbeth].

KING.   See, see, our honour'd hostess!   10
The love that follows us sometime is our trouble,
Which still we thank as love. Herein I teach you
How you shall bid God 'ield us for your pains
And thank us for your trouble.

LADY.   All our service
In every point twice done, and then done double,   15
Were poor and single business to contend
Against those honours deep and broad wherewith

I.VI. 1 *seat* site.   1–3 *The air . . . senses* the air, by its freshness and sweetness,
appeals pleasantly to our senses and makes them gentle — soothes them.   4
martlet the house martin, called "temple-haunting" because it often builds about
churches [K] (ROWE; F¹: "Barlet").   *approve* prove.   5 *By . . . mansionry* by the
fact that he has chosen this as a favourite site for his mansions [K] (F¹: "Man-
sonry").   6 *wooingly* so as to appeal to the senses by its delightful freshness [K].
jutty projection.   7 *coign of vantage* advantageous corner or angle.   8 *procreant
cradle* cradle where he breeds.   9 *most* ROWE; F¹: "must."   11–12 *The love . . .
as love* the love that sometimes gives us trouble (by forcing attention upon us)
we nevertheless are grateful for.   13 *God 'ield us* God repay me.   14–20 *All our
service . . . hermits* Duncan has paid Lady Macbeth a formal but skillfully turned
compliment in the taste of the Elizabethan time. Her reply is equally graceful.

Your Majesty loads our house. For those of old,
And the late dignities heap'd up to them,
We rest your hermits.

KING.   Where's the Thane of Cawdor?   20
We cours'd him at the heels and had a purpose
To be his purveyor; but he rides well,
And his great love, sharp as his spur, hath holp him
To his home before us. Fair and noble hostess,
We are your guest to-night.

LADY.   Your servants ever   25
Have theirs, themselves, and what is theirs, in compt,
To make their audit at your Highness' pleasure,
Still to return your own.

KING.   Give me your hand;
Conduct me to mine host. We love him highly
And shall continue our graces towards him.   30
By your leave, hostess.   *Exeunt.*

◆◆◆◆◆◆◆◆◆◆◆◆◆◆◆◆◆

SCENE VII. [*Inverness. Macbeth's Castle.*]

Hautboys. Torches. Enter a Sewer, *and divers* Servants
    with dishes and service over the stage. Then enter
    Macbeth.

MACB.   If it were done when 'tis done, then 'twere well
It were done quickly. If th' assassination
Could trammel up the consequence, and catch,

Her ceremonious style is in fine contrast to Duncan's gracious badinage [K].
16 *single* insignificant.   16–17 *contend Against* offset.   19 *late* recent.   20
hermits beadsmen, those who pray for your well-being.   21 *cours'd* pursued.
22 *purveyor* literally, an officer who precedes a king or great noble when on a
journey and makes arrangements for provisions and other supplies [K].   23 *holp*
helped.   26 *theirs* their servants. *what is theirs* their possessions. *in compt* not
as their own property, but as something entrusted to them by you [K].   27 *make
their audit* render their account.   28 *Still* always, at any moment. She means
that everything she and her husband have is really the King's and that he has the
right to call for it, or any part of it, at any time [K].   30 *graces* royal favours.
    I.VII. s.d. *Sewer* chief waiter.   3 *Could . . . consequence* could catch (as in a
trammel or net) that which may follow (and so prevent its occurrence) [K].

With his surcease, success; that but this blow
Might be the be-all and the end-all here,   5
But here, upon this bank and shoal of time,
We'ld jump the life to come. But in these cases
We still have judgment here, that we but teach
Bloody instructions, which, being taught, return
To plague th' inventor. This even-handed justice   10
Commends th' ingredience of our poison'd chalice
To our own lips. He's here in double trust:
First, as I am his kinsman and his subject —
Strong both against the deed; then, as his host,
Who should against his murderer shut the door,   15
Not bear the knife myself. Besides, this Duncan
Hath borne his faculties so meek, hath been
So clear in his great office, that his virtues
Will plead like angels, trumpet-tongu'd, against
The deep damnation of his taking-off;   20
And pity, like a naked new-born babe,
Striding the blast, or heaven's cherubin, hors'd
Upon the sightless couriers of the air,
Shall blow the horrid deed in every eye,
That tears shall drown the wind. I have no spur   25
To prick the sides of my intent, but only
Vaulting ambition, which o'erleaps itself
And falls on th' other side.

Enter Lady [Macbeth].

How now? What news?

LADY.   He has almost supp'd. Why have you left the chamber?

---

4 *his surcease* Duncan's death.   6 *shoal* THEOBALD; F¹: "Schoole."   7 *jump . . .
come* risk afterlife.   8 *still* always. *here* in this world.   8–10 *that we . . . inventor* so that he who murders a king in order to get the crown is teaching others how
to murder him for the same purpose [K].   11 *Commends* applies. *ingredience*
elements composing the draught in the chalice [K].   17 *borne his faculties* exer-
cised his power. *so meek* so mildly.   18 *clear* blameless.   21 *like* in the form of.
22 *Striding the blast* riding the wind.   23 *sightless couriers* invisible steeds, i.e.
the winds.   25 *drown the wind* as heavy rain is said to do [K].   25–8 *I have . . .
side* Ambition, first thought of as a "spur," becomes the horseman who, meaning
to vault into the saddle, springs too high and falls disgracefully [K]. *side* HANMER;

MACB.   Hath he ask'd for me?

LADY.   Know you not he has?   30

MACB.   We will proceed no further in this business.
         He hath honour'd me of late, and I have bought
         Golden opinions from all sorts of people,
         Which would be worn now in their newest gloss,
         Not cast aside so soon.

LADY.   Was the hope drunk   35
         Wherein you dress'd yourself? Hath it slept since?
         And wakes it now to look so green and pale
         At what it did so freely? From this time
         Such I account thy love. Art thou afeard
         To be the same in thine own act and valour   40
         As thou art in desire? Wouldst thou have that
         Which thou esteem'st the ornament of life,
         And live a coward in thine own esteem,
         Letting "I dare not" wait upon "I would,"
         Like the poor cat i' th' adage?

MACB.   Prithee peace!   45
         I dare do all that may become a man.
         Who dares do more is none.

LADY.   What beast was't then
         That made you break this enterprise to me?
         When you durst do it, then you were a man;
         And to be more than what you were, you would   50
         Be so much more the man. Nor time nor place
         Did then adhere, and yet you would make both.

---

not in F¹.   38 *freely* without compulsion.   42 *ornament of life* life's chief adorn-
ment — the crown [K].   43 *live a coward* do without it, and always accuse yourself
of cowardice when you think of the opportunity you have lost [K].   *esteem*
opinion.   44 *wait upon* constantly attend.   45 *th' adage* The cat would eat fish
but would not wet her feet. The proverb appears in many forms.   47 *do more*
ROWE; F¹: "no more."   48 *break* propose.   50–1 *And to be . . . man* and by being
more daring than you were then — by daring to do what you then dared to resolve
— you would be even more the man than you then were [K].   51–2 *Nor time . . .*
both there was then no suitable time or place for the murder, and you were then
willing to create opportunity (for the murder).

They have made themselves, and that their fitness now
Does unmake you. I have given suck, and know
How tender 'tis to love the babe that milks me.   55
I would, while it was smiling in my face,
Have pluck'd my nipple from his boneless gums
And dash'd the brains out, had I so sworn as you
Have done to this.

MACB.   If we should fail?

LADY.   We fail?
But screw your courage to the sticking place,   60
And we'll not fail. When Duncan is asleep
(Whereto the rather shall his day's hard journey
Soundly invite him), his two chamberlains
Will I with wine and wassail so convince
That memory, the warder of the brain,   65
Shall be a fume, and the receipt of reason
A limbeck only. When in swinish sleep
Their drenched natures lie as in a death,
What cannot you and I perform upon
Th' unguarded Duncan? what not put upon   70
His spongy officers, who shall bear the guilt
Of our great quell?

MACB.   Bring forth men-children only;
For thy undaunted mettle should compose
Nothing but males. Will it not be receiv'd,
When we have mark'd with blood those sleepy two   75
Of his own chamber and us'd their very daggers,
That they have done't?

---

53 *have made themselves* time and place are now provided by Duncan's visit.
that their fitness that very fitness of time and place [к].   54 *unmake*
unman.   60 *screw . . . sticking place* The figure is from a crossbow or arbalest.
The bow was made of steel, and a mechanical device, sometimes worked with
a crank, was attached to the barrel of the gun, by means of which the bow
was bent. When fully screwed up, the bowstring would catch in a notch (the
"sticking place") and the weapon was ready to discharge [к].   64 *wassail* carous-
ing. *convince* overpower completely.   65-7 *memory . . . only* According to the
old physiology, memory resided in the base of the brain at the back of the skull,

LADY.   Who dares receive it other,
          As we shall make our griefs and clamour roar
          Upon his death?

MACB.   I am settled and bend up
          Each corporal agent to this terrible feat.   80
          Away, and mock the time with fairest show;
          False face must hide what the false heart doth know.

                                                    Exeunt.

just above the neck, and reason in the upper part below the dome of the head.
The fumes of wine were thought to rise from the stomach to the brain and thus
to cause drunkenness [K].   67 *limbeck* the alembic, or cap of the still, into which
the fumes rise in the process of distillation [K].   68 *drenched* drowned.   *lie* F²;
F¹: "lyes."   71 *spongy* drunken, soaking up drink like a sponge.   72 *quell*
murder.   73 *mettle* substance, quality.   79 *settled* resolute.   79 *bend up* stretch
tight (like a bow).   80 *corporal* bodily.   81 *mock the time* beguile the world.
show appearance.

Act Two

◇◇◇◇◇◇◇◇◇◇◇◇◇◇◇◇◇◇◇◇◇◇◇◇◇◇◇◇◇◇◇◇◇◇◇◇◇◇

SCENE I.
[Inverness. Court of Macbeth's *Castle.]*

Enter Banquo, *and* Fleance *with a torch before him.*

BAN. How goes the night, boy?

FLE. The moon is down; I have not heard the clock.

BAN. And she goes down at twelve.

FLE.   I take't, 'tis later, sir.

BAN. Hold, take my sword. There's husbandry in heaven;
Their candles are all out. Take thee that too.   5
A heavy summons lies like lead upon me,
And yet I would not sleep. Merciful powers,
Restrain in me the cursed thoughts that nature
Gives way to in repose!

Enter Macbeth, *and a* Servant *with a torch.*

                              Give me my sword.
Who's there?   10

II.1. 4 *husbandry* economy, frugality.   5 *candles* the stars.   *that too* probably
his dagger.   6 *heavy summons* drowsiness, a summons to sleep.   8–9 *cursed
thoughts . . . repose* Disagreeable and evil thoughts were supposed to be put into
men's minds during the helplessness of the will in slumber [K].   14 *largess* gifts.
offices servants' quarters where the household work was performed.   16–17 *shut
up . . . content* concluded what he had to say with expressions of unmeasured
satisfaction at your hospitality [K], or ended his day in contentment.   18–19 *Our
will . . . wrought* our wish to entertain the King sumptuously (which otherwise

MACB.   A friend.

BAN.   What, sir, not yet at rest? The King's abed.
        He hath been in unusual pleasure and
        Sent forth great largess to your offices.
        This diamond he greets your wife withal   15
        By the name of most kind hostess, and shut up
        In measureless content.

MACB.   Being unprepar'd,
        Our will became the servant to defect,
        Which else should free have wrought.

BAN.   All's well.
        I dreamt last night of the three Weird Sisters.   20
        To you they have show'd some truth.

MACB.   I think not of them.
        Yet when we can entreat an hour to serve,
        We would spend it in some words upon that business,
        If you would grant the time.

BAN.   At your kind'st leisure.

MACB.   If you shall cleave to my consent, when 'tis,   25
        It shall make honour for you.

BAN.   So I lose none
        In seeking to augment it but still keep
        My bosom franchis'd and allegiance clear,
        I shall be counsell'd.

MACB.   Good repose the while!

BAN.   Thanks, sir. The like to you!   30

                    Exeunt Banquo [*and* Fleance].

MACB.   Go bid thy mistress, when my drink is ready,

---

would have had free play) was hampered by lack of due preparation [K].   **20**
Weird (F¹: "weyward").   **25** *cleave to my consent* join my party; espouse my
interests [K].   **26** *So* provided that.   **27** *still* always.   **28** *franchis'd* free from
blame.   **29** *I shall be counsell'd* I shall be ready to follow your suggestion.   **31**
drink the regular draught of warm spiced wine or the like which every Elizabethan
or medieval gentleman and lady took just before going to bed. Such a draught
was thought to be eminently wholesome [K].

She strike upon the bell. Get thee to bed.

Exit [Servant].

Is this a dagger which I see before me,
The handle toward my hand? Come, let me clutch thee!
I have thee not, and yet I see thee still.   35
Art thou not, fatal vision, sensible
To feeling as to sight? or art thou but
A dagger of the mind, a false creation,
Proceeding from the heat-oppressed brain?
I see thee yet, in form as palpable   40
As this which now I draw.
Thou marshall'st me the way that I was going,
And such an instrument I was to use.
Mine eyes are made the fools o' th' other senses,
Or else worth all the rest. I see thee still;   45
And on thy blade and dudgeon gouts of blood,
Which was not so before. There's no such thing.
It is the bloody business which informs
Thus to mine eyes. Now o'er the one half-world
Nature seems dead, and wicked dreams abuse   50
The curtain'd sleep. Witchcraft celebrates
Pale Hecate's offerings; and wither'd murder,
Alarum'd by his sentinel, the wolf,
Whose howl's his watch, thus with his stealthy pace,
With Tarquin's ravishing strides, towards his design   55
Moves like a ghost. Thou sure and firm-set earth,

33–49 *Is this . . . mine eyes* This famous soliloquy shows once more the highly
imaginative nature of Macbeth, which visualizes to the verge of delirium [K].
36 *fatal* sent by fate. *sensible* perceptible by the senses.   44–5 *Mine eyes . . .
rest* my eyes have become fools (because they are deluded and see what does not
exist) in comparison with my other senses (which are under no such delusion);
or else, if the dagger is real, my eyes (which alone perceive it) are worth all my
other senses together [K].   46 *dudgeon* wooden hilt. *gouts* big drops. 48 *informs*
gives (false) information [K].   50 *abuse* deceive.   51 *curtain'd sleep* sleeper in
his curtained bed [K].   51 *Witchcraft* F¹; DAVENANT, K: "Now witchcraft."   52
Hecate's offerings sacrifices to Hecate, the classical goddess of witchcraft.   53
Alarum'd summoned to action [K].   54 *watch* When the wolf howls, the murderer
knows that the time has come for him to act. Hence the howl of the wolf is the
murderer's timepiece, striking the hour [K].   55 *strides* long steps (POPE; F¹:
"sides").   56 *sure* CAPELL; F¹: "sowre."   57 *way they* ROWE; F¹: "they may."

Hear not my steps which way they walk, for fear
Thy very stones prate of my whereabout
And take the present horror from the time,
Which now suits with it. Whiles I threat, he lives;   60
Words to the heat of deeds too cold breath gives.

           A bell rings.

I go, and it is done. The bell invites me.
Hear it not, Duncan, for it is a knell
That summons thee to heaven, or to hell.   *Exit.*

❖❖❖❖❖❖❖❖❖❖❖❖

SCENE II. [*Inverness.* Macbeth's *Castle.*]

Enter Lady [Macbeth].

LADY.   That which hath made them drunk hath made me bold;
        What hath quench'd them hath given me fire. Hark!
           Peace!
        It was the owl that shriek'd, the fatal bellman
        Which gives the stern'st good-night. He is about it.
        The doors are open, and the surfeited grooms   5
        Do mock their charge with snores. I have drugg'd their
           possets,
        That death and nature do contend about them
        Whether they live or die.

MACB.   [*within*] Who's there? What, ho?

---

59 *present horror* the dreadful silence which suits the time and the purpose, and which Macbeth wishes should not be disturbed by the sound of his steps [K]. 60-1 *Whiles . . . gives* talking tends to postpone action that should be carried out in the heat of resolution [K].

II.II. 3 *fatal bellman* It was the custom in London for the bellman or town-crier to visit condemned prisoners on the night before their execution [K]. In 1604 one Robert Dow, a London merchant, gave a fund so that the bell of St. Sepulcher's Church near Newgate prison might be tolled on nights before executions, the bellman also to ring a handbell outside the cells of condemned prisoners at midnight so that they might think of their sins.   4 *stern'st good-night* The owl's hoot portends death, according to a superstition not yet extinct [K].   5 *surfeited* overfed.   6 *mock their charge* make a mockery of their duty. *possets* bedtime drinks.

LADY.	Alack, I am afraid they have awak'd, 10
	And 'tis not done! Th' attempt, and not the deed,
	Confounds us. Hark! I laid their daggers ready;
	He could not miss 'em. Had he not resembled
	My father as he slept, I had done't.

Enter Macbeth.

My husband!

MACB.	I have done the deed. Didst thou not hear a noise? 15
LADY.	I heard the owl scream and the crickets cry.
	Did not you speak?
MACB.	When?
LADY.	Now.
MACB.	As I descended?
LADY.	Ay.
MACB.	Hark!
	Who lies i' th' second chamber?
LADY.	Donalbain. 20
MACB.	This is a sorry sight. [*Looks on his hands.*]
LADY.	A foolish thought, to say a sorry sight.
MACB.	There's one did laugh in's sleep, and one cried "Murder!"
	That they did wake each other. I stood and heard them.
	But they did say their prayers and address'd them 25
	Again to sleep.
LADY.	There are two lodg'd together.
MACB.	One cried "God bless us!" and "Amen!" the other,
	As they had seen me with these hangman's hands,
	List'ning their fear. I could not say "Amen!"

---

12 *Confounds* ruins.   21 *sorry* miserable.   25 *address'd them* applied themselves.
28 *hangman's hands* bloody like those of the executioner (hangman), whose duty
it was to tear the vital organs out of his victims before cutting their bodies to
pieces.   29 *their fear* to their fearful prayers.   33 *thought* thought upon, regarded [K].   34 *After these ways* in such a fashion as this (with an agonized
dwelling on every little detail, and perplexity as to what it means) [K].   *So if we
do so.*   37 *knits up* untangles and straightens out.   *ravell'd* tangled, snarled.

When they did say "God bless us!"

LADY.   Consider it not so deeply.   30

MACB.   But wherefore could not I pronounce "Amen"?
I had most need of blessing, and "Amen"
Stuck in my throat.

LADY.   These deeds must not be thought
After these ways. So, it will make us mad.

MACB.   Methought I heard a voice cry "Sleep no more!   35
Macbeth does murder sleep." — the innocent sleep,
Sleep that knits up the ravell'd sleave of care,
The death of each day's life, sore labour's bath,
Balm of hurt minds, great nature's second course,
Chief nourisher in life's feast.

LADY.   What do you mean?   40

MACB.   Still it cried "Sleep no more!" to all the house;
"Glamis hath murder'd sleep, and therefore Cawdor
Shall sleep no more! Macbeth shall sleep no more!"

LADY.   Who was it that thus cried? Why, worthy Thane,
You do unbend your noble strength to think   45
So brainsickly of things. Go get some water
And wash this filthy witness from your hand.
Why did you bring these daggers from the place?
They must lie there. Go carry them and smear
The sleepy grooms with blood.

MACB.   I'll go no more.   50
I am afraid to think what I have done;
Look on't again I dare not.

LADY.   Infirm of purpose!
Give me the daggers. The sleeping and the dead

---

sleave skein (STEEVENS; F¹: "sleeve").   38 *bath* because it cures weariness, like a
warm bath after toil [K].   39-40 *second course . . . life's feast* Life's feast has
two courses — food and sleep. Macbeth regards the second as even more sustaining
to our nature than the first. The second course was the most substantial part of
an Elizabethan dinner [K].   45 *unbend* relax.   47 *witness* evidence.   53-4 *The
sleeping . . . pictures* the sleeping and the dead are only pictures of living men,
and pictures cannot hurt you [K].

Are but as pictures. 'Tis the eye of childhood
That fears a painted devil. If he do bleed,   55
I'll gild the faces of the grooms withal,
For it must seem their guilt.

Exit. Knocking within.

MACB.   Whence is that knocking?
How is't with me when every noise appals me?
What hands are here? Ha! they pluck out mine eyes!
Will all great Neptune's ocean wash this blood   60
Clean from my hand? No. This my hand will rather
The multitudinous seas incarnadine,
Making the green one red.

Enter Lady [Macbeth].

LADY.   My hands are of your colour, but I shame
To wear a heart so white. (*Knock.*) I hear a knocking   65
At the south entry. Retire we to our chamber.
A little water clears us of this deed.
How easy is it then! Your constancy
Hath left you unattended. (*Knock.*) Hark! more knocking.
Get on your nightgown, lest occasion call us   70
And show us to be watchers. Be not lost
So poorly in your thoughts.

MACB.   To know my deed, 'twere best not know myself.   *Knock.*
Wake Duncan with thy knocking! I would thou couldst!
                                                    Exeunt.

---

56 *gild* stain or smear with blood.   62 *The multitudinous seas* all the seas of the
world with their multitude of tumbling waves [κ].   *incarnadine* make red.   63
Making . . . red turning the green colour of the seas into one universal red, or
"total gules" [κ].   66 *entry* entrance.   68–9 *Your . . . unattended* your customary
firmness has abandoned you.   70 *nightgown* dressing gown.   70–1 *lest occasion
. . . watchers* lest something cause us to be summoned and reveal that we have
not been in bed.   72 *poorly* weakly.   73 *To know . . . myself* if consciousness
means that I must look my crime in the face, I would rather be unconscious
forever.

II.III. 2 *old* a great deal of (a common colloquial expression).   4–5 *farmer
. . . plenty* The farmer had held his wheat for a high price, regardless of the
needs of the poor. But the next crop seemed likely to be heavy, and, desperate at

◆◇◆◇◆◇◆◇◆◇◆◇◆◇◆◇

SCENE III. [*Inverness.* Macbeth's *Castle.*]

Enter a Porter. *Knocking within.*

PORTER. Here's a knocking indeed! If a man were porter of hell
gate, he should have old turning the key. (*Knock.*) Knock,
knock, knock! Who's there, i' th' name of Belzebub?
Here's a farmer that hang'd himself on th' expectation
of plenty. Come in time! Have napkins enow about you;   5
here you'll sweat for't. (*Knock*). Knock, knock! Who's
there, in th' other devil's name? Faith, here's an equivocator, that could swear in both the scales against either
scale; who committed treason enough for God's sake, yet
could not equivocate to heaven. O, come in, equivocator!   10
(*Knock.*) Knock, knock, knock! Who's there? Faith, here's
an English tailor come hither for stealing out of a French
hose. Come in, tailor. Here you may roast your goose.
(*Knock.*) Knock, knock! Never at quiet! What are you?
But this place is too cold for hell. I'll devil-porter it no   15
further. I had thought to have let in some of all profes-
sions that go the primrose way to th' everlasting bonfire.
(*Knock.*) Anon, anon! [*Opens the gate.*] I pray you remember the porter.

Enter Macduff *and* Lennox.

MACD. Was it so late, friend, ere you went to bed,   20
That you do lie so late?

---

the prospect of a drop in prices, he committed suicide. Such speculating in food-
stuffs has been a favourite subject for denunciation ever since the Middle Ages
[K]. *napkins* handkerchiefs. *enow* enough.   7 *equivocator* A fling at the Jesuits,
who were believed to justify deceptive ambiguity and "mental reservations" [K].
8–9 *swear . . . scale* make an ambiguous statement and swear on it; swear to a
form of words that has two meanings, so that, whichever way the oath is understood by the hearer, the swearer can say to himself that he meant the other thing
[K].   12–13 *tailor . . . hose* Tailors were proverbially said to steal cloth in the
process of cutting out clothes for their customers. The kind of French hose
(breeches) here intended was tight-fitting and required little cloth. It would take
a skillful thief, therefore, to embezzle any [K].   13 *goose* tailor's pressing iron.
15 *devil-porter it* act the part of a demon porter at hell gate [K].

PORT.	Faith, sir, we were carousing till the second cock; and drink, sir, is a great provoker of three things.
MACD.	What three things does drink especially provoke?
PORT.	Marry, sir, nose-painting, sleep, and urine. Lechery, sir, 25 it provokes, and unprovokes: it provokes the desire, but it takes away the performance. Therefore much drink may be said to be an equivocator with lechery: it makes him, and it mars him; it sets him on, and it takes him off; it persuades him, and disheartens him; makes him 30 stand to, and not stand to; in conclusion, equivocates him in a sleep, and, giving him the lie, leaves him.
MACD.	I believe drink gave thee the lie last night.
PORT.	That it did, sir, i' the very throat on me; but I requited him for his lie; and, I think, being too strong for him, 35 though he took up my legs sometime, yet I made a shift to cast him.
MACD.	Is thy master stirring?

Enter Macbeth.

	Our knocking has awak'd him; here he comes.
LEN.	Good morrow, noble sir.
MACB.	Good morrow, both. 40
MACD.	Is the King stirring, worthy Thane?
MACB.	Not yet.
MACD.	He did command me to call timely on him; I have almost slipp'd the hour.
MACB.	I'll bring you to him.

---

22 *second cock* 3 A.M.   33 *gave thee the lie* (a) floored you, as in wrestling (b) sent you sound asleep (c) lied to you.   34 *throat on me* To lie in one's throat was to tell a deep or deliberate lie, as opposed to a mere lip falsehood. The porter's pun is obvious [K].   *requited* repaid.   36 *took up my legs* succeeded in getting my feet off the ground. The figure is from wrestling [K].   *made a shift* contrived. 37 *cast* (a) throw (b) vomit.   42 *timely* early.   46 *labour . . . pain* when any kind of labour gives us pleasure, the pleasure relieves all the effort that the labour involves [K].   48 *limited service* specially appointed duty.   49 *appoint* arrange.   52 *Lamentings . . . death* Such prodigies were regularly supposed to

MACD.   I know this is a joyful trouble to you;
        But yet 'tis one.   45

MACB.   The labour we delight in physics pain.
        This is the door.

MACD.   I'll make so bold to call,
        For 'tis my limited service.   *Exit.*

LEN.   Goes the King hence to-day?

MACB.   He does; he did appoint so.

LEN.   The night has been unruly. Where we lay,   50
        Our chimneys were blown down; and, as they say,
        Lamentings heard i' th' air, strange screams of death,
        And prophesying, with accents terrible,
        Of dire combustion and confus'd events
        New hatch'd to th' woeful time. The obscure bird   55
        Clamour'd the livelong night. Some say the earth
        Was feverous and did shake.

MACB.   'Twas a rough night.

LEN.   My young remembrance cannot parallel
        A fellow to it.

                    Enter Macduff.

MACD.   O horror, horror, horror! Tongue nor heart   60
        Cannot conceive nor name thee!

MACB. AND LEN.   What's the matter?

MACD.   Confusion now hath made his masterpiece!
        Most sacrilegious murder hath broke ope
        The Lord's anointed temple and stole thence

---

announce or accompany the death of princes or great men [K].   54 *combustion*
tumult and disorder.   55 *obscure bird* the owl, bird of darkness.   57 *feverous*
Malarial fever (fever and ague) was prevalent in Shakespeare's England, for there
were immense undrained marshes, and the chills and shaking that accompany it
are often used in metaphor [K].   62 *Confusion* destruction.   64 *The Lord's
anointed temple* the sacred body of the King, which is not only God's temple,
but God's anointed temple. Our bodies are God's temples according to the passage
in 2 CORINTHIANS, VI, 16 [K].

The life o' th' building!

MACB.   What is't you say? the life?   65

LEN.   Mean you his Majesty?

MACD.   Approach the chamber, and destroy your sight
With a new Gorgon. Do not bid me speak.
See, and then speak yourselves.

Exeunt Macbeth *and* Lennox.

Awake, awake!
Ring the alarum bell. Murder and treason!   70
Banquo and Donalbain! Malcolm! awake!
Shake off this downy sleep, death's counterfeit,
And look on death itself! Up, up, and see
The great doom's image! Malcolm! Banquo!
As from your graves rise up and walk like sprites   75
To countenance this horror! Ring the bell!   *Bell rings*

Enter Lady [Macbeth].

LADY.   What's the business,
That such a hideous trumpet calls to parley
The sleepers of the house? Speak, speak!

MACD.   O gentle lady,
'Tis not for you to hear what I can speak!   80
The repetition in a woman's ear
Would murder as it fell.

Enter Banquo.

O Banquo, Banquo,
Our royal master's murder'd!

LADY.   Woe, alas!
What, in our house?

---

68 *Gorgon* The horrible sight will, like the Gorgon Medusa, turn his eyes to stone
[K].   72 *counterfeit* imitation, likeness.   74 *great doom's image* a sight as dreadful as the Day of Doom [K].   75 *As from your graves* The doomsday comparison
is continued. *like sprites* as spirits.   76 *countenance* (a) keep the horrid sight in
countenance; that is, to accord with it, to give it a proper setting [K] (b) look
upon.   81 *repetition* recital.   89 *serious* worth while. *mortality* human life.
90 *toys* trifles.   91-2 *The wine . . . brag of* everything that gave zest to existence
is gone, now that Duncan is dead, and this world (like an empty wine vault) has

BAN.   Too cruel anywhere.
         Dear Duff, I prithee contradict thyself   85
         And say it is not so.

                    Enter Macbeth, Lennox, *and* Ross

MACB.   Had I but died an hour before this chance,
         I had liv'd a blessed time; for from this instant
         There's nothing serious in mortality;
         All is but toys; renown and grace is dead;   90
         The wine of life is drawn, and the mere lees
         Is left this vault to brag of.

                    Enter Malcolm *and* Donalbain.

DON.   What is amiss?

MACB.   You are, and do not know't.
         The spring, the head, the fountain of your blood
         Is stopp'd, the very source of it is stopp'd.   95

MACD.   Your royal father's murder'd.

MAL.   O, by whom?

LEN.   Those of his chamber, as it seem'd, had done't.
         Their hands and faces were all badg'd with blood;
         So were their daggers, which unwip'd we found
         Upon their pillows.   100
         They star'd and were distracted. No man's life
         Was to be trusted with them.

MACB.   O, yet I do repent me of my fury
         That I did kill them.

MACD.   Wherefore did you so?

MACB.   Who can be wise, amaz'd, temp'rate and furious,   105

---

nothing left of its vaunted pleasures — nothing but the nauseous dregs of life [K].
94 *head* well-head or source.   98 *badg'd* marked. The figure comes from the
badges or cognizances which retainers of great houses were accustomed to wear.
These consisted usually of the arms or crest of the head of the house [K].   103
fury madness, frenzy (not wrath) [K].   105 *amaz'd* utterly confused in mind,
mentally paralyzed (not, as in modern English, surprised) [K].   *temp'rate* self-
controlled.   *furious* frenzied.

Loyal and neutral, in a moment? No man.
The expedition of my violent love
Outrun the pauser, reason. Here lay Duncan,
His silver skin lac'd with his golden blood,
And his gash'd stabs look'd like a breach in nature   110
For ruin's wasteful entrance; there, the murderers,
Steep'd in the colours of their trade, their daggers
Unmannerly breech'd with gore. Who could refrain
That had a heart to love and in that heart
Courage to make's love known?

LADY.   Help me hence, ho!   115

MACD.   Look to the lady.

MAL.   [*aside to* Donalbain] Why do we hold our tongues,
That most may claim this argument for ours?

DON.   [*aside to* Malcolm] What should be spoken here, where
          our fate,
Hid in an auger hole, may rush and seize us?
Let's away.   120
Our tears are not yet brew'd.

MAL.   [*aside to* Donalbain]   Nor our strong sorrow
Upon the foot of motion.

BAN.   Look to the lady.

                    [Lady Macbeth *is carried out.*]

And when we have our naked frailties hid,
That suffer in exposure, let us meet

---

107 *expedition* haste.   109 *lac'd* interlaced, streaked.   110 *a breach* The figure
is of a city wall in which assailants have made a breach by which they can enter
and lay waste the town [K].   111 *wasteful* destructive.   113 *Unmannerly breech'd*
covered (as by breeches) in an unseemly fashion. *refrain* hold back.   117 *That
most . . . ours* who have most right to talk about this subject (argument).   119
Hid . . . hole lurking in some unsuspected hiding place [K], so small as a hole
made by an auger.   121 *tears . . . brew'd* the time has not come for us to weep
for our father [K].   121–2 *Nor . . . motion* nor has our grief, strong as it is, yet
begun to act — it is felt, not shown [K].   123 *naked frailties hid* clothed our
naked bodies.   126 *scruples* vague suspicions.   128 *undivulg'd pretence* as

And question this most bloody piece of work,   125
To know it further. Fears and scruples shake us.
In the great hand of God I stand, and thence
Against the undivulg'd pretence I fight
Of treasonous malice.

MACD.   And so do I.

ALL.   So all.

MACB. Let's briefly put on manly readiness   130
And meet i' th' hall together.

ALL.   Well contented.

                    Exeunt [*all but* Malcolm *and* Donalbain].

MAL.   What will you do? Let's not consort with them.
To show an unfelt sorrow is an office
Which the false man does easy. I'll to England.

DON.   To Ireland I. Our separated fortune   135
Shall keep us both the safer. Where we are,
There's daggers in men's smiles; the near in blood,
The nearer bloody.

MAL.   This murderous shaft that's shot
Hath not yet lighted, and our safest way
Is to avoid the aim. Therefore to horse!   140
And let us not be dainty of leave-taking
But shift away. There's warrant in that theft
Which steals itself when there's no mercy left.   *Exeunt.*

---

yet undiscovered purpose of the traitor (whoever he is) who has contrived this
foul deed [K].   130 *briefly* quickly.   *put on manly readiness* clothe ourselves
properly (not, put on our armour) [K].   132 *consort* associate.   133 *office* function.
135 *Our . . . fortune* this separation for our fortune; the fact that we try our
luck separately [K].   137-8 *the near . . . bloody* the nearer one of these nobles
is to us in kindred, the more likely he is to wish to murder us [K].   138-9 *This
. . . lighted* this arrow of murder is still in the air; this murderous plot has not
yet attained its full object (our death as well as our father's) [K].   141 *dainty of*
punctilious about.   142 *shift away* steal away unseen.   *warrant* justification.

◇◇◇◇◇◇◇◇◇◇◇◇◇◇◇◇◇◇

SCENE IV. [*Inverness. Without* Macbeth's *Castle.*]

Enter Ross *with an* Old Man.

OLD MAN. Threescore and ten I can remember well;
Within the volume of which time I have seen
Hours dreadful and things strange; but this sore night
Hath trifled former knowings.

ROSS.   Ha, good father,
Thou seest the heavens, as troubled with man's act,   5
Threatens his bloody stage. By th' clock 'tis day,
And yet dark night strangles the travelling lamp.
Is't night's predominance, or the day's shame,
That darkness does the face of earth entomb
When living light should kiss it?

OLD MAN.   'Tis unnatural,   10
Even like the deed that's done. On Tuesday last
A falcon, tow'ring in her pride of place,
Was by a mousing owl hawk'd at and kill'd.

ROSS. And Duncan's horses (a thing most strange and certain),
Beauteous and swift, the minions of their race,   15
Turn'd wild in nature, broke their stalls, flung out,
Contending 'gainst obedience, as they would make
War with mankind.

OLD MAN.   'Tis said they eat each other.

ROSS. They did so, to th' amazement of mine eyes
That look'd upon't.

II.IV. 3 *sore* dreadful.   4 *trifled former knowings* made former experiences
seem trivial.   *Ha* F¹; ROWE, K: "Ah."   6 *Threatens* F¹; ROWE, K: "Threaten."
bloody stage this earth, on which man performs his bloody deeds [K]. The theatrical analogy is common in Shakespeare.   7 *travelling lamp* of Phoebus, the sun.
8–10 *Is't . . . kiss it* is the darkness due to Night's having become more powerful
in the world than Day, or to Day's hiding his face in shame? [K].   12 *tow'ring
. . . place* soaring proudly, and at the very summit (or highest pitch) of her flight
[K].   13 *mousing owl* owl, whose natural prey is mice, not falcons [K].   *hawk'd at*
swooped upon.   15 *minions* darlings.   16 *flung out* kicked and plunged wildly.

Enter Macduff.

Here comes the good Macduff.   20
How goes the world, sir, now?

MACD.   Why, see you not?

ROSS.   Is't known who did this more than bloody deed?

MACD.   Those that Macbeth hath slain.

ROSS.   Alas, the day!
What good could they pretend?

MACD.   They were suborn'd.
Malcolm and Donalbain, the King's two sons,   25
Are stol'n away and fled, which puts upon them
Suspicion of the deed.

ROSS.   'Gainst nature still!
Thriftless ambition, that wilt raven up
Thine own life's means! Then 'tis most like
The sovereignty will fall upon Macbeth.   30

MACD.   He is already nam'd, and gone to Scone
To be invested.

ROSS.   Where is Duncan's body?

MACD.   Carried to Colmekill,
The sacred storehouse of his predecessors
And guardian of their bones.

ROSS.   Will you to Scone?   35

MACD.   No, cousin, I'll to Fife.

ROSS.   Well, I will thither.

---

18 *eat* ate.   19 *amazement* stupefaction.   24 *pretend* expect to gain.   *suborn'd*
bribed or induced.   28 *Thriftless* improvident.   *wilt* WARBURTON; F[1]: "will."
raven up devour ravenously. In their mad ambition to reign they have destroyed
all their own prospects of succeeding to the throne [K].   29 *like* likely.   31 *nam'd*
elected.   *Scone* where the Scottish kings were regularly crowned [K].   32 *invested*
clothed with sovereignty (at the coronation) [K].   33 *Colmekill* Columba's cell —
the island now usually called Iona, where St. Columba had a monastery and where
he and the ancient Scottish kings were buried [K].

MACD.   Well, may you see things well done there. Adieu,
        Lest our old robes sit easier than our new!

ROSS.   Farewell, father.

OLD MAN. God's benison go with you, and with those   40
        That would make good of bad, and friends of foes!

                                      Exeunt omnes.

40–1 *God's benison . . . foes* God's blessing go with you both — and with all other well-meaning and unsuspicious persons who, like you, insist on regarding bad men as good and your foes as your friends [K].

Act Three

◇◇◇

SCENE I. [*Forres. The Palace.*]

Enter Banquo.

BAN. Thou hast it now — King, Cawdor, Glamis, all,
As the Weird Women promis'd; and I fear
Thou play'dst most foully for't. Yet it was said
It should not stand in thy posterity,
But that myself should be the root and father   5
Of many kings. If there come truth from them,
(As upon thee, Macbeth, their speeches shine),
Why, by the verities on thee made good,
May they not be my oracles as well
And set me up in hope? But, hush, no more!   10

> Sennet *sounded. Enter* Macbeth, *as*
> King; Lady [Macbeth, *as* Queen]; Len-
> nox, Ross, Lords, *and* Attendants.

MACB. Here's our chief guest.

LADY.   If he had been forgotten,
It had been as a gap in our great feast,
And all-thing unbecoming.

MACB. To-night we hold a solemn supper, sir,
And I'll request your presence.

III.I. 3 *foully* treacherously.   4 *stand* continue as a legacy.   7 *shine* are brilliantly
fulfilled.   13 *all-thing* altogether.   14 *solemn supper* state supper, official
banquet.

BAN.   Let your Highness   15
        Command upon me, to the which my duties
        Are with a most indissoluble tie
        For ever knit.

MACB.   Ride you this afternoon?

BAN.   Ay, my good lord.   20

MACB.   We should have else desir'd your good advice
        (Which still hath been both grave and prosperous)
        In this day's council; but we'll take to-morrow.
        Is't far you ride?

BAN.   As far, my lord, as will fill up the time   25
        'Twixt this and supper. Go not my horse the better,
        I must become a borrower of the night
        For a dark hour or twain.

MACB.   Fail not our feast.

BAN.   My lord, I will not.

MACB.   We hear our bloody cousins are bestow'd   30
        In England and in Ireland, not confessing
        Their cruel parricide, filling their hearers
        With strange invention. But of that to-morrow,
        When therewithal we shall have cause of state
        Craving us jointly. Hie you to horse. Adieu,   35
        Till you return at night. Goes Fleance with you?

BAN.   Ay, my good lord. Our time does call upon's.

MACB.   I wish your horses swift and sure of foot,
        And so I do commend you to their backs.
        Farewell.   *Exit* Banquo. 40

---

22 *still* always. *grave and prosperous* weighty and good in its results. Note the
implication that there have been previous councils: Macbeth has now reigned for
some time [K].   26–8 *Go not . . . twain* unless my horse goes too fast to make
that necessary, I shall have to continue my ride an hour or two after dark [K].
30 *cousins* Malcolm and Donalbain. *are bestow'd* have taken refuge.   33 *strange
invention* false tales; they have been accusing Macbeth of the murder.   34 *cause
of state* public affairs.   35 *Craving us jointly* requiring both your attention and
mine. Thus Macbeth associates himself with Banquo in a very particular manner,
as if they had common interests which the others did not share. Banquo may well
think that the business meant is the prophecy made by the Weird Sisters to him

Let every man be master of his time
Till seven at night. To make society
The sweeter welcome, we will keep ourself
Till supper time alone. While then, God be with you!

> *Exeunt* Lords [*and others. Manent*
> Macbeth *and a* Servant].

Sirrah, a word with you. Attend those men   45
Our pleasure?

SERV.   They are, my lord, without the palace gate.

MACB.   Bring them before us.   *Exit* Servant.

                    To be thus is nothing,
But to be safely thus. Our fears in Banquo
Stick deep; and in his royalty of nature   50
Reigns that which would be fear'd. 'Tis much he dares,
And to that dauntless temper of his mind
He hath a wisdom that doth guide his valour
To act in safety. There is none but he
Whose being I do fear; and under him   55
My Genius is rebuk'd, as it is said
Mark Antony's was by Cæsar. He chid the Sisters
When first they put the name of King upon me,
And bade them speak to him. Then, prophet-like,
They hail'd him father to a line of kings.   60
Upon my head they plac'd a fruitless crown
And put a barren sceptre in my gripe,
Thence to be wrench'd with an unlineal hand,
No son of mine succeeding. If't be so,
For Banquo's issue have I fil'd my mind;   65

[K].   42–4 *To make . . . alone* in order that company (your society) may be all
the more agreeable to me, I will deprive myself of it for a time [K].   45 *Sirrah*
a term used to address servants or inferiors. *Attend* await.   48 *thus* King.
49 *But* unless.   50 *Stick deep* are deeply rooted (in me).   51 *would be* deserves
to be.   52 *to* in addition to. *temper* quality, disposition.   56 *Genius* controlling
or guardian spirit. *rebuk'd* put to shame.   57 *Mark Antony's was by Cæsar*
Plutarch reports that an Egyptian soothsayer told Antony that his fortune would
be obscured by that of Octavius Cæsar so long as he remained in his company.
62 *gripe* grasp.   63 *with* by.   65 *fil'd* defiled.

For them the gracious Duncan have I murder'd;
Put rancours in the vessel of my peace
Only for them, and mine eternal jewel
Given to the common enemy of man
To make them kings, the seeds of Banquo kings!   70
Rather than so, come, Fate, into the list,
And champion me to th' utterance! Who's there?

Enter Servant *and two* Murderers.

Now go to the door and stay there till we call.

Exit Servant.

Was it not yesterday we spoke together?

MURDERERS. It was, so please your Highness.

MACB.   Well then, now   75
Have you consider'd of my speeches? Know
That it was he, in the times past, which held you
So under fortune, which you thought had been
Our innocent self. This I made good to you
In our last conference, pass'd in probation with you   80
How you were borne in hand, how cross'd; the
        instruments;
Who wrought with them; and all things else that might
To half a soul and to a notion craz'd
Say "Thus did Banquo."

1. MUR.   You made it known to us.

MACB. I did so; and went further, which is now   85
Our point of second meeting. Do you find
Your patience so predominant in your nature

---

67 *rancours* malignant enmities. The figure is of a vessel full of some wholesome liquid (like milk) into which poison has been poured [K].   68 *eternal
jewel* immortal soul.   69 *common enemy of man* Satan.   70 *seeds* F¹; POPE,
K: "seed."   71 *list* the lists, place of combat.   72 *champion me* meet me
face to face in combat.   *to th' utterance* "à l'outrance," a chivalric term meaning
combat to the uttermost, to death.   77 *he* Banquo.   77–8 *held you . . . fortune*
kept you out of favour with fortune, thwarted your careers.   79 *made good*
proved.   80 *pass'd in probation* reviewed the evidence.   81 *borne in hand*
deluded (by Banquo). To bear a man in hand is not merely to deceive him, but
to do so by means of a regular course of treachery; to play the hypocrite with
him; to nourish false hopes, etc. [K].   *cross'd* thwarted. *instruments* tools.   83
half a soul half-wit. *notion* intellect.   86 *point* purpose.   87 *patience* passive

That you can let this go? Are you so gospell'd
To pray for this good man and for his issue,
Whose heavy hand hath bow'd you to the grave   90
And beggar'd yours for ever?

1. MUR.   We are men, my liege.

MACB.   Ay, in the catalogue ye go for men,
As hounds and greyhounds, mongrels, spaniels, curs,
Shoughs, water-rugs, and demi-wolves are clept
All by the name of dogs. The valued file   95
Distinguishes the swift, the slow, the subtle,
The housekeeper, the hunter, every one
According to the gift which bounteous nature
Hath in him clos'd; whereby he does receive
Particular addition, from the bill   100
That writes them all alike; and so of men.
Now, if you have a station in the file,
Not i' th' worst rank of manhood, say't;
And I will put that business in your bosoms
Whose execution takes your enemy off,   105
Grapples you to the heart and love of us,
Who wear our health but sickly in his life,
Which in his death were perfect.

2. MUR.   I am one, my liege,
Whom the vile blows and buffets of the world
Hath so incens'd that I am reckless what   110
I do to spite the world.

1. MUR.   And I another,
So weary with disasters, tugg'd with fortune,

---

endurance.   88 *gospell'd* tamely submissive to the gospel injunction to love your
enemies (MATTHEW, v, 44).   91 *yours* your families.   92 *the catalogue* a mere list.
go for pass for.   94 *Shoughs* a kind of shaggy Iceland dog, in favour as a lady's
pet in Shakespeare's time [K].   *water-rugs* some kind of shaggy water-dog [K].
demi-wolves a cross between wolf and dog [K].   *clept* called (CAPELL; F¹, K: "clipt").
95 *valued file* the list which (as opposed to an indiscriminate catalogue) notes the
valuable quality which distinguishes each breed [K].   97 *housekeeper* watchdog.
99 *in him clos'd* endowed him with.   100–1 *Particular . . . alike* a special name
or title, in distinction from the list ("bill") that writes them all down indis-
criminately as dogs [K].   107 *wear . . . life* have but feeble health so long as he
is alive (since his life endangers mine) [K].   110 *Hath* F¹; K: "Have."   112
tugg'd with pulled about by.

That I would set my life on any chance,
To mend it or be rid on't.

MACB.   Both of you
Know Banquo was your enemy.

MURDERERS.   True, my lord.   115

MACB.   So is he mine; and in such bloody distance
That every minute of his being thrusts
Against my near'st of life; and though I could
With barefac'd power sweep him from my sight
And bid my will avouch it, yet I must not,   120
For certain friends that are both his and mine,
Whose loves I may not drop, but wail his fall
Who I myself struck down. And thence it is
That I to your assistance do make love,
Masking the business from the common eye   125
For sundry weighty reasons.

2. MUR.   We shall, my lord,
Perform what you command us.

1. MUR.   Though our lives —

MACB.   Your spirits shine through you. Within this hour at most
I will advise you where to plant yourselves,
Acquaint you with the perfect spy o' th' time,   130
The moment on't; for't must be done to-night,
And something from the palace; always thought
That I require a clearness; and with him,
To leave no rubs nor botches in the work,
Fleance his son, that keeps him company,   135
Whose absence is no less material to me
Than is his father's, must embrace the fate

---

113 *set* stake.   *chance* hazard.   116 *bloody distance* mortal enmity.   118
near'st of life most vital spot. Banquo's mere existence is a dagger, set at
Macbeth's breast over his heart and pressed so steadily and inexorably minute
by minute [K].   119 *barefac'd power* open display of royal authority.   120
avouch authorize, justify.   121 *For* because of.   122 *wail* I must lament.
130 *with . . . time* with absolutely full and exact indication of the time
when the deed should be done [K].   132 *something* some distance.   *thought*

Of that dark hour. Resolve yourselves apart;
I'll come to you anon.

MURDERERS.   We are resolv'd, my lord.

MACB.   I'll call upon you straight. Abide within.

> [*Exeunt* Murderers.]   140

It is concluded. Banquo, thy soul's flight,
If it find heaven, must find it out to-night.   *Exit.*

◇◇◇◇◇◇◇◇◇◇◇◇◇◇◇

SCENE II. [*Forres. The Palace.*]

Enter Macbeth's Lady *and a* Servant.

LADY.   Is Banquo gone from court?

SERV.   Ay, madam, but returns again to-night.

LADY.   Say to the King I would attend his leisure
For a few words.

SERV.   Madam, I will.   *Exit.*

LADY.   Naught's had, all's spent,
Where our desire is got without content.   5
'Tis safer to be that which we destroy
Than by destruction dwell in doubtful joy.

Enter Macbeth.

How now, my lord? Why do you keep alone,
Of sorriest fancies your companions making,
Using those thoughts which should indeed have died   10
With them they think on? Things without all remedy
Should be without regard. What's done is done.

---

borne in mind.   133 *clearness* freedom from suspicion, alibi.   134 *rubs*
impediments.   *botches* defects due to bungling.   138 *Resolve yourselves apart*
make up your minds, by conferring in private, whether you will undertake the
business or not [K].   140 *straight* immediately.

III.II.   5 *content* happiness.   9 *sorriest fancies* most despicable thoughts.   10
Using associating with. The word carries out the figure of the preceding verse
[K].   11 *without* beyond.   12 *regard* concern.

MACB.	We have scorch'd the snake, not kill'd it.	
	She'll close, and be herself, whilst our poor malice	
	Remains in danger of her former tooth.	15
	But let the frame of things disjoint, both the worlds suffer,	
	Ere we will eat our meal in fear and sleep	
	In the affliction of these terrible dreams	
	That shake us nightly. Better be with the dead,	
	Whom we, to gain our peace, have sent to peace,	20
	Than on the torture of the mind to lie	
	In restless ecstasy. Duncan is in his grave;	
	After life's fitful fever he sleeps well.	
	Treason has done his worst. Nor steel nor poison,	
	Malice domestic, foreign levy, nothing,	25
	Can touch him further.	
LADY.	Come on.	
	Gentle my lord, sleek o'er your rugged looks;	
	Be bright and jovial among your guests to-night.	
MACB.	So shall I, love; and so, I pray, be you.	
	Let your remembrance apply to Banquo;	30
	Present him eminence both with eye and tongue —	
	Unsafe the while, that we	
	Must lave our honours in these flattering streams	
	And make our faces vizards to our hearts,	
	Disguising what they are.	

---

13 *scorch'd* slashed with a knife, and thus wounded only slightly (F¹; THEOBALD, κ: "scotch'd"). There is no real need for the emendation, although it has been widely accepted.   14 *close* come together again; join and be as strong as ever. It was a common notion (not yet obsolete) that a snake, when cut in two, will reunite unless the head is crushed [κ].   14-15 *our poor . . . tooth* our feeble enmity has proved of no avail and leaves us exposed to the same danger (from the serpent) as when it was uninjured [κ].   16 *let . . . disjoint* may the structure of the universe collapse. *both the worlds* heaven and earth. *suffer* perish.   20 *gain our peace* secure our own happiness.   21 *on . . . lie* to find that our bed is a rack on which we are stretched in torment [κ].   22 *restless ecstasy* a frenzy of sleeplessness and unrest [κ].   25 *Malice domestic* civil war. *foreign levy* invasion from abroad.   27 *sleek o'er* smooth over. *rugged* agitated; literally, rough, shaggy [κ].   30 *Let . . . Banquo* remember to show particular attention to Banquo [κ].   31 *Present him eminence* do special honour to him.   32 *Unsafe . . . that* we are unsafe so long as.   33 *Must lave . . . streams* must wash the honours that we have in streams of flattery to keep them clean. A grotesque and violent figure

LADY.   You must leave this.   35

MACB.   O, full of scorpions is my mind, dear wife!
         Thou know'st that Banquo, and his Fleance, lives.

LADY.   But in them Nature's copy's not eterne.

MACB.   There's comfort yet! They are assailable.
         Then be thou jocund. Ere the bat hath flown   40
         His cloister'd flight, ere to black Hecate's summons
         The shard-borne beetle with his drowsy hums
         Hath rung night's yawning peal, there shall be done
         A deed of dreadful note.

LADY.   What's to be done?

MACB.   Be innocent of the knowledge, dearest chuck,   45
         Till thou applaud the deed. Come, seeling night,
         Scarf up the tender eye of pitiful day,
         And with thy bloody and invisible hand
         Cancel and tear to pieces that great bond
         Which keeps me pale! Light thickens, and the crow   50
         Makes wing to th' rooky wood.
         Good things of day begin to droop and drowse,
         Whiles night's black agents to their preys do rouse.
         Thou marvell'st at my words; but hold thee still:
         Things bad begun make strong themselves by ill.   55
         So prithee go with me.   *Exeunt.*

---

which shows the impatient self-contempt of the speaker. The thought is that, to
retain their position, they must court the favour of Banquo and the rest [K].   34
vizards masks.   38 *But . . . eterne* Nature has granted them, not a perpetual
lease of life, but a mere copyhold tenure, easy to revoke or to terminate [K].
40-1 *bat . . . cloister'd* The bat's flight is not, like a bird's in the open air, but
in belfries and cloisters — in darkness and solitude [K].   41-3 *ere . . . peal* ere
the droning beetle, in obedience to Hecate's summons, has announced the coming
of drowsy night [K] *shard-borne* (a) borne on scaly wings (b) dung-bred.   44
dreadful note dreadful to be known.   46 *seeling* To "seel" is to sew up the eye-
lids (of a falcon) with silk — to keep it in the dark and tame it [K].   47 *Scarf up*
blindfold.   49 *bond* This has been variously explained: (a) the prophecy by
which Fate has bound itself to give the throne to Banquo's descendents [K] (b)
Banquo's lease on life (c) the bond of Nature which links Macbeth to the rest of
humanity and endows him with human feeling.   50 *thickens* grows dim.   51
rooky (a) harbouring rooks (b) misty, gloomy — from "roke," an old term for
"smoke."

◇◇◇◇◇◇◇◇◇◇◇◇◇◇◇◇

SCENE III. [*Forres. A park near the Palace.*]

Enter three Murderers.

1. MUR. But who did bid thee join with us?

3. MUR.   Macbeth.

2. MUR. He needs not our mistrust, since he delivers
Our offices, and what we have to do,
To the direction just.

1. MUR.   Then stand with us.
The west yet glimmers with some streaks of day.   5
Now spurs the lated traveller apace
To gain the timely inn, and near approaches
The subject of our watch.

3. MUR.   Hark! I hear horses.

BAN. (*within*) Give us a light there, ho!

2. MUR.   Then 'tis he! The rest
That are within the note of expectation   10
Already are i' th' court.

1. MUR.   His horses go about.

3. MUR. Almost a mile; but he does usually,
So all men do, from hence to th' palace gate
Make it their walk.

                    Enter Banquo, *and* Fleance *with a
                    torch.*

2. MUR.   A light, a light!

III.III. 1 We hear only the end of the dialogue. The Third Murderer has given
the other two the information which Macbeth had promised to send them (III.I.
128–31) and has proved that he is in the King's confidence by repeating such
directions as they had already received. Some critics imagine that this Third
Murderer was Macbeth himself. If this were so, the interview between Macbeth
and the First Murderer (III.IV.12*ff*) would lose all its force and become not only
useless but absurd [K]. Shakespeare probably introduced the Third Murderer to
show that Macbeth, like any tyrant, cannot trust his underlings but must spy even

3. MUR.	'Tis he.
1. MUR.	Stand to't. 15
BAN.	It will be rain to-night.
1. MUR.	Let it come down!

[They fall upon Banquo.]

BAN.	O, treachery! Fly, good Fleance, fly, fly, fly! Thou mayst revenge. O slave! *[Dies. Fleance escapes.]*
3. MUR.	Who did strike out the light?
1. MUR.	Was't not the way?
3. MUR.	There's but one down; the son is fled.
2. MUR.	We have lost 20 Best half of our affair.
1. MUR.	Well, let's away, and say how much is done. *Exeunt.*

◇◇◇◇◇◇◇◇◇◇◇◇◇◇◇◇

SCENE IV. [*Forres. Hall in the Palace.*]

Banquet prepar'd. Enter Macbeth, Lady [Macbeth],
Ross, Lennox, Lords, *and* Attendants.

MACB.	You know your own degrees, sit down. At first And last the hearty welcome.
LORDS.	Thanks to your Majesty.
MACB.	Ourself will mingle with society And play the humble host. Our hostess keeps her state, but in best time 5

---

upon them.   2 *delivers* reports.   3 *offices* duties.   4 *To the direction just* according to our exact instructions.   6 *lated* belated.   7 *To gain . . . inn* to reach
the inn in good season (before it is quite dark) [K].   *and* F²; F¹: "end."   8 *subject*
object.   10 *within . . . expectation* in the list of expected guests [K].   19 *way*
proper thing to do.

   III.IV. 1 *degrees* ranks, and hence the seat which each should take [K].   1–2
At first And last at the beginning and the end of the supper; once for all [K].
5 *keeps her state* sits on her chair of state.   *in best time* at the proper moment.

We will require her welcome.

LADY.   Pronounce it for me, sir, to all our friends,
For my heart speaks they are welcome.

Enter First Murderer [*to the door*].

MACB.   See, they encounter thee with their hearts' thanks.
Both sides are even. Here I'll sit i' th' midst.   10
Be large in mirth; anon we'll drink a measure
The table round. [*Goes to the door.*] There's blood upon
          thy face.

MUR.   'Tis Banquo's then.

MACB.   'Tis better thee without than he within.
Is he dispatch'd?   15

MUR.   My lord, his throat is cut. That I did for him.

MACB.   Thou art the best o' th' cutthroats! Yet he's good
That did the like for Fleance. If thou didst it,
Thou art the nonpareil.

MUR.   Most royal sir,
Fleance is scap'd.   20

MACB.   [*aside*] Then comes my fit again. I had else been perfect;
Whole as the marble, founded as the rock,
As broad and general as the casing air.
But now I am cabin'd, cribb'd, confin'd, bound in
To saucy doubts and fears. — But Banquo's safe?   25

MUR.   Ay, my good lord. Safe in a ditch he bides,
With twenty trenched gashes on his head,
The least a death to nature.

MACB.   Thanks for that!

---

9 *encounter* respond to.   10 *even* equally filled.   11 *large in mirth* unrestrained,
lavish in enjoyment.   *measure* large goblet.   14 *'Tis . . . within* it's better that
the blood should be outside of thee than inside of Banquo [K].   19 *nonpareil*
paragon.   21 *fit* of feverous anxiety.   22 *founded* firmly established.   23 *casing*
all-embracing.   24 *cabin'd, cribb'd* shut up in a cabin — nay, in a mere hut [K].
24–5 *bound . . . fears* shut in, with no companions but importunate doubts and
fears (that force themselves upon me and will not let me alone) [K].   *safe* disposed
of.   27 *trenched* deep-cut.   29 *worm* small serpent.   32 *hear ourselves* talk
with each other.   33 *cheer* tokens of hospitality.   33–5 *The feast . . . welcome*

There the grown serpent lies; the worm that's fled
Hath nature that in time will venom breed,   30
No teeth for th' present. Get thee gone. Tomorrow
We'll hear ourselves again.   *Exit* Murderer.

LADY.   My royal lord,
You do not give the cheer. The feast is sold
That is not often vouch'd, while 'tis a-making,
'Tis given with welcome. To feed were best at home.   35
From thence, the sauce to meat is ceremony;
Meeting were bare without it.

           Enter the Ghost of Banquo, *and sits
           in* Macbeth's *place.*

MACB.   Sweet remembrancer!
Now good digestion wait on appetite,
And health on both!

LEN.   May't please your Highness sit.

MACB.   Here had we now our country's honour, roof'd,   40
Were the grac'd person of our Banquo present;
Who may I rather challenge for unkindness
Than pity for mischance!

ROSS.   His absence, sir,
Lays blame upon his promise. Please't your Highness
To grace us with your royal company?   45

MACB.   The table's full.

LEN.   Here is a place reserv'd, sir.

MACB.   Where?

LEN.   Here, my good lord. What is't that moves your Highness?

Unless the host's words and demeanour assure his guests that they are welcome, he might as well be an innkeeper [K]. *vouch'd* certified. *feed* eat merely to satisfy hunger.   36 *From thence . . . ceremony* away from home, courtesy (ceremony) is the sauce which lends flavour to the food (meat).   38 *wait on* attend. 40 *had we . . . roof'd* we should now have all the noblest men of Scotland under one roof [K].   41 *grac'd* honoured.   42–3 *Who may . . . mischance* whom I hope I should rather blame for unkindness (in staying away on purpose) than pity for some accident (that has prevented his coming) [K].   48 *moves* disturbs.

MACB.   Which of you have done this?

LORDS.   What, my good lord?

MACB.   Thou canst not say I did it. Never shake   50
         Thy gory locks at me.

ROSS.   Gentlemen, rise. His Highness is not well.

LADY.   Sit, worthy friends. My lord is often thus,
         And hath been from his youth. Pray you keep seat.
         The fit is momentary; upon a thought   55
         He will again be well. If much you note him,
         You shall offend him and extend his passion.
         Feed, and regard him not. — Are you a man?

MACB.   Ay, and a bold one, that dare look on that
         Which might appal the devil.

LADY.   O proper stuff!   60
         This is the very painting of your fear.
         This is the air-drawn dagger which you said
         Led you to Duncan. O, these flaws and starts
         (Impostors to true fear) would well become
         A woman's story at a winter's fire,   65
         Authoriz'd by her grandam. Shame itself!
         Why do you make such faces? When all's done,
         You look but on a stool.

MACB.   Prithee see there! behold! look! lo! How say you?
         Why, what care I? If thou canst nod, speak too.   70
         If charnel houses and our graves must send
         Those that we bury back, our monuments

---

49 *done this* either (a) killed Banquo or (b) put the corpse in the chair.   51 *gory locks* The long hair of the apparition is matted with blood from the "twenty trenched gashes" [K].   55 *upon a thought* in a moment.   57 *offend him* make him worse. *passion* suffering.   62 *air-drawn* unsheathed and floating in the air — with a contemptuous implication of unreality, as if drawn (delineated) by the air [K].   63 *flaws* outbursts. *starts* nervous movements.   64 *Impostors . . . fear* mere tricks of the nerves, unworthy to be called genuine fear. They are like the shudders with which children listen to a ghost story, safely gathered round the cottage fire [K].   66 *Authoriz'd* vouched for. The woman who tells the old wife's tale can cite only her grandmother as authority [K].   68 *You . . . stool* The ghost is visible only to Macbeth.   71 *charnel houses.* A charnel house was a vault

Shall be the maws of kites.

[*Exit* Ghost.]

LADY.   What, quite unmann'd in folly?

MACB.   If I stand here, I saw him.

LADY.   Fie, for shame!

MACB.   Blood hath been shed ere now, i' th' olden time,   75
Ere humane statute purg'd the gentle weal;
Ay, and since too, murders have been perform'd
Too terrible for the ear. The time has been
That, when the brains were out, the man would die,
And there an end! But now they rise again,   80
With twenty mortal murders on their crowns,
And push us from our stools. This is more strange
Than such a murder is.

LADY.   My worthy lord,
Your noble friends do lack you.

MACB.   I do forget.
Do not muse at me, my most worthy friends.   85
I have a strange infirmity, which is nothing
To those that know me. Come, love and health to all!
Then I'll sit down. Give me some wine, fill full.

Enter Ghost.

I drink to th' general joy o' th' whole table,
And to our dear friend Banquo, whom we miss.   90
Would he were here! To all, and him, we thirst,
And all to all.

LORDS.   Our duties, and the pledge.

---

or small building attached to a church and used as a storehouse for such skulls
and bones as came to light in digging new graves [K].   72–3 *our monuments . . .
kites* the dead shall be thrown out in the open fields to be devoured by birds of
prey, and thus the only monuments we allow them shall be the bellies of kites
[K].   76 *Ere . . . weal* before civilizing law cleansed society (of primeval savagery)
and made it gentle (i.e. in the old times of lawless barbarism) [K].   77 *since too*
even since that time.   78 *time* GRANT WHITE; F¹: "times."   81 *mortal murders*
deadly wounds.   *crowns* heads.   84 *lack you* miss your company.   85 *muse*
wonder, be astonished.   91 *To all . . . thirst* I am eager to drink to you all, and
to Banquo in particular [K].   92 *all to all* everybody (drink) to everybody.

MACB.   Avaunt, and quit my sight! Let the earth hide thee!
        Thy bones are marrowless, thy blood is cold;
        Thou hast no speculation in those eyes   95
        Which thou dost glare with!

LADY.   Think of this, good peers,
        But as a thing of custom. 'Tis no other.
        Only it spoils the pleasure of the time.

MACB.   What man dare, I dare.
        Approach thou like the rugged Russian bear,   100
        The arm'd rhinoceros, or th' Hyrcan tiger;
        Take any shape but that, and my firm nerves
        Shall never tremble. Or be alive again
        And dare me to the desert with thy sword.
        If trembling I inhabit then, protest me   105
        The baby of a girl. Hence, horrible shadow!
        Unreal mock'ry, hence!   [*Exit* Ghost.]
                           Why, so! Being gone,
        I am a man again. Pray you sit still.

LADY.   You have displac'd the mirth, broke the good meeting
        With most admir'd disorder.

MACB.   Can such things be,   110
        And overcome us like a summer's cloud
        Without our special wonder? You make me strange
        Even to the disposition that I owe,
        When now I think you can behold such sights
        And keep the natural ruby of your cheeks   115

---

95 *speculation* intelligent sight. The ghost's eyes are like a dead man's — fixed in a glassy stare [K].   97 *custom* common occurrence.   100 *like* in the shape of. *rugged* shaggy and fierce. *Russian bear* Bears were imported from Russia for the bear-baiting at Paris Garden [K].   101 *Hyrcan* from Hyrcania, an ancient region south of the Caspian Sea.   104 *desert* some solitary place, for a duel to the death without seconds or witnesses [K].   105 *If trembling . . . then* if then, as now I live in terror [K].   106 *baby of a girl* the child of a very young mother — and so, "a timid weakling." This is far more likely than the alternative — "a girl's doll" [K]. Others have suggested "a baby girl."   107 *mock'ry* illusion.   110 *admir'd* wondered at.   *disorder* distracted behaviour.   111–12 *overcome . . . wonder* come over us as suddenly as a cloud in summer, and yet excite no more surprise than such a cloud [K].   112–13 *You . . . owe* you make me feel that I

When mine is blanch'd with fear.

ROSS.   What sights, my lord?

LADY.   I pray you speak not. He grows worse and worse;
          Question enrages him. At once, good night.
          Stand not upon the order of your going,
          But go at once.

LEN.   Good night, and better health   120
          Attend his Majesty!

LADY.   A kind good night to all!
                             Exeunt Lords [*and* Attendants].

MACB.   It will have blood, they say; blood will have blood.
          Stones have been known to move and trees to speak;
          Augures and understood relations have
          By maggot-pies and choughs and rooks brought forth   125
          The secret'st man of blood. What is the night?

LADY.   Almost at odds with morning, which is which.

MACB.   How say'st thou that Macduff denies his person
          At our great bidding?

LADY.   Did you send to him, sir?

MACB.   I hear it by the way; but I will send.   130
          There's not a one of them but in his house
          I keep a servant fee'd. I will to-morrow
          (And betimes I will) unto the Weird Sisters.
          More shall they speak; for now I am bent to know

---

do not know my own nature, which I had supposed to be that of a brave man
[K]. *owe* own.   118 *enrages* drives into a frenzy.   119 *Stand . . . going* do not
be punctilious about precedence as you leave the hall. Under ordinary circum-
stances the nobles would depart slowly and ceremoniously, in the order of their
rank [K].   123-6 *Stones . . . blood* Macbeth recalls various instances in which
murders have been miraculously brought to light. The theory was that murder is
so atrocious in God's eyes that he will not suffer it to go undetected [K].   124
Augures auguries, signs from the flight of birds [K].   *understood relations* reports
properly comprehended [K].   125 *maggot-pies* magpies.   *choughs* jackdaws (a
kind of crow).   *brought forth* revealed.   127 *at odds* at variance.   130 *by the
way* incidentally.   132 *feed* paid by me (for spying).   133 *betimes* at once.
Weird (F[1]: "weyward").   134 *bent* determined.

By the worst means the worst. For mine own good   135
All causes shall give way. I am in blood
Stepp'd in so far that, should I wade no more,
Returning were as tedious as go o'er.
Strange things I have in head, that will to hand,
Which must be acted ere they may be scann'd.   140

LADY.   You lack the season of all natures, sleep.

MACB.   Come, we'll to sleep. My strange and self-abuse
Is the initiate fear that wants hard use.
We are yet but young in deed.   *Exeunt.*

◆◆◆◆◆◆◆◆◆◆◆◆◆◆◆◆◆◆

SCENE V. [*A heath.*]

Thunder. Enter the three Witches, *meeting* Hecate.

1. WITCH. Why, how now, Hecate? You look angerly.

HEC.   Have I not reason, beldams as you are,
Saucy and overbold? How did you dare
To trade and traffic with Macbeth
In riddles and affairs of death;   5
And I, the mistress of your charms,
The close contriver of all harms,
Was never call'd to bear my part
Or show the glory of our art?
And, which is worse, all you have done   10
Hath been but for a wayward son,

---

136 *causes* considerations   139 *to hand* be executed.   140 *scann'd* examined.   141
season preservative; that without which no living creature can remain sound and
normal [K].   142 *strange and self-abuse* strange delusion.   143 *initiate* fear felt
by a novice in crime, the implication being that when he has had more experience
as a murderer he will have no such delusions.   143 *hard use* practice that hardens
one.   144 *in deed* THEOBALD; F¹: "indeed."
    III.v. This scene is probably a non-Shakespearean interpolation.   2 *beldams*

Spiteful and wrathful, who, as others do,
Loves for his own ends, not for you.
But make amends now. Get you gone
And at the pit of Acheron   15
Meet me i' th' morning. Thither he
Will come to know his destiny.
Your vessels and your spells provide,
Your charms and everything beside.
I am for th' air. This night I'll spend   20
Unto a dismal and a fatal end.
Great business must be wrought ere noon.
Upon the corner of the moon
There hangs a vap'rous drop profound.
I'll catch it ere it come to ground;   25
And that, distill'd by magic sleights,
Shall raise such artificial sprites
As by the strength of their illusion
Shall draw him on to his confusion.
He shall spurn fate, scorn death, and bear   30
His hopes 'bove wisdom, grace, and fear;
And you all know security
Is mortals' chiefest enemy.

> *Music and a song within.* "Come away,
> come away," &c.

Hark! I am call'd. My little spirit, see,
Sits in a foggy cloud and stays for me.   *[Exit.]* 35

1. WITCH. Come, let's make haste. She'll soon be back again.

> *Exeunt.*

---

hags.   7 *close* secret.   11 *wayward* perverse.   15 *Acheron* Certainly it is not to
Acheron (a river of the infernal regions) that Macbeth comes to seek the witches,
but to a Scottish cavern [K].   21 *dismal* disastrous.   24 *vap'rous drop profound*
a drop of condensed vapour, deep-hanging, pear-shaped, and so about to fall [K].
26 *sleights* secret arts (F¹: "slights").   27 *artificial sprites* spirits produced by
magic.   29 *confusion* destruction.   31 *grace* virtue.   32 *security* overconfidence.

◇◇◇◇◇◇◇◇◇◇◇◇◇◇◇◇◇

SCENE VI. [*Forres. The Palace.*]

Enter Lennox *and another* Lord.

LEN.   My former speeches have but hit your thoughts,
Which can interpret farther. Only I say
Things have been strangely borne. The gracious Duncan
Was pitied of Macbeth. Marry, he was dead!
And the right valiant Banquo walk'd too late;   5
Whom, you may say (if't please you) Fleance kill'd,
For Fleance fled. Men must not walk too late.
Who cannot want the thought how monstrous
It was for Malcolm and for Donalbain
To kill their gracious father? Damned fact!   10
How it did grieve Macbeth! Did he not straight,
In pious rage, the two delinquents tear,
That were the slaves of drink and thralls of sleep?
Was not that nobly done? Ay, and wisely too!
For 'twould have anger'd any heart alive   15
To hear the men deny't. So that I say
He has borne all things well; and I do think
That, had he Duncan's sons under his key
(As, an't please heaven, he shall not), they should find
What 'twere to kill a father. So should Fleance.   20
But peace! for from broad words, and 'cause he fail'd
His presence at the tyrant's feast, I hear
Macduff lives in disgrace. Sir, can you tell
Where he bestows himself?

LORD.   The son of Duncan,
From whom this tyrant holds the due of birth,   25

III.vi. 1 *hit your thoughts* agreed with what you have been thinking.   2 *interpret farther* draw further conclusions.   3 *borne* managed.   4 *of* by. *was dead*
Macbeth pitied Duncan after he was dead, but not before [K].   8 *want the thought*
help but think.   10 *fact* evil deed.   11 *straight* immediately.   12 *delinquents*
offenders.   13 *thralls* slaves.   19 *an't* if it.   21 *from broad words* because of
too free or unguarded speech.   22 *tyrant's* usurper's.   24 *bestows himself* has
taken refuge. *son* THEOBALD; F¹: "Sonnes."   25 *holds* withholds. *due of birth*
birthright.   27 *Edward* Edward the Confessor, King of England from 1042 to

Lives in the English court, and is receiv'd
Of the most pious Edward with such grace
That the malevolence of fortune nothing
Takes from his high respect. Thither Macduff
Is gone to pray the holy King upon his aid　30
To wake Northumberland and warlike Siward;
That by the help of these (with Him above
To ratify the work) we may again
Give to our tables meat, sleep to our nights,
Free from our feasts and banquets bloody knives,　35
Do faithful homage and receive free honours —
All which we pine for now. And this report
Hath so exasperate the King that he
Prepares for some attempt of war.

LEN.　　　　　　　　　　　　Sent he to Macduff?

LORD.　He did; and with an absolute "Sir, not I!"　40
The cloudy messenger turns me his back
And hums, as who should say, "You'll rue the time
That clogs me with this answer."

LEN.　　　　　　　　　　　　And that well might
Advise him to a caution t' hold what distance
His wisdom can provide. Some holy angel　45
Fly to the court of England and unfold
His message ere he come, that a swift blessing
May soon return to this our suffering country
Under a hand accurs'd!

LORD.　　　　　　　　　　I'll send my prayers with him.

Exeunt.

1066. *grace* favour.　29 *respect* regard with which he is held.　30 *upon his aid*
for his assistance.　31 *wake* call to arms. *Northumberland* the people of that
region. *Siward* Earl of Northumberland.　34 *meat* food.　36 *faithful* sincere.
free unconstrained; granted with good will on the King's part. At present their
homage to Macbeth is insincere, and the honour that he shows them in return is
not voluntary (free) because it is the result of fear [K].　37 *this report* of the
favour shown to Malcolm.　38 *the King* HANMER; F¹: "then King."　41 *cloudy*
with a clouded face, frowning.　43 *clogs me* makes me return with reluctant feet
[K].　46 *unfold* disclose.　48-9 *our . . . Under* our country, suffering under.

Act Four

◆◇◆

SCENE I.
[A cavern. In the middle, a cauldron boiling.]

Thunder. Enter the three Witches.

1. WITCH. Thrice the brinded cat hath mew'd.

2. WITCH. Thrice and once the hedge-pig whin'd.

3. WITCH. Harpier cries; 'tis time, 'tis time.

1. WITCH. Round about the cauldron go;
In the poison'd entrails throw.   5
Toad, that under cold stone
Days and nights has thirty-one
Swelt'red venom sleeping got,
Boil thou first i' th' charmed pot.

ALL.   Double, double, toil and trouble;   10
Fire burn, and cauldron bubble.

2. WITCH. Fillet of a fenny snake,
In the cauldron boil and bake;
Eye of newt, and toe of frog,
Wool of bat, and tongue of dog,   15

IV.I. 1 *brinded* brindled, striped.   2 *hedge-pig* hedgehog.   3 *Harpier* a familiar spirit, suggested by "harpy."   8 *Swelt'red* coming out in drops, like sweat [K]. *sleeping got* formed while sleeping.   12 *Fillet* slice. *fenny* swamp.   16 *blind-worm* a small snakelike lizard erroneously supposed to be sightless. Though not in fact venomous, it is still popularly regarded as dangerous [K].   17 *howlet* small owl.   23 *Witch's mummy* mummified fragment of a witch. Human flesh was thought to be powerful in magic — especially the flesh of criminals, of non-Christians, or of persons who had met with a violent death or had not had Christian burial [K].   *maw* stomach. *gulf* gullet.   24 *ravin'd* ravenous.   25 *i'*

Adder's fork, and blindworm's sting,
Lizard's leg, and howlet's wing;
For a charm of pow'rful trouble
Like a hell-broth boil and bubble.

ALL.   Double, double, toil and trouble;   20
Fire burn, and cauldron bubble.

3. WITCH. Scale of dragon, tooth of wolf
Witch's mummy, maw and gulf
Of the ravin'd salt-sea shark,
Root of hemlock, digg'd i' th' dark;   25
Liver of blaspheming Jew,
Gall of goat, and slips of yew
Sliver'd in the moon's eclipse;
Nose of Turk and Tartar's lips;
Finger of birth-strangled babe   30
Ditch-deliver'd by a drab:
Make the gruel thick and slab.
Add thereto a tiger's chaudron
For th' ingredience of our cauldron.

ALL.   Double, double, toil and trouble;   35
Fire burn, and cauldron bubble.

2. WITCH. Cool it with a baboon's blood,
Then the charm is firm and good.

Enter Hecate *to the other three*
Witches.

HEC.   O, well done! I commend your pains,
And every one shall share i' th' gains.
And now about the cauldron sing   40

---

th' dark The time when an herb was gathered was supposed to affect its potency in medicine [K].   27 *yew* tree associated with graveyards and thought to be poisonous.   28 *Sliver'd* sliced. *eclipse* a particularly ill-omened time [K].   30 *birth-strangled* strangled as soon as born, and hence not baptized. Infants who died unchristened were the object of many superstitions. Sometimes they were thought to haunt the earth as a kind of demon. In any case, their flesh was regarded as powerful in evil spells [K].   31 *Ditch-deliver'd* born in a ditch. *drab* harlot.   32 *slab* thick, viscous.   33 *chaudron* entrails.   34 *ingredience* composition.

> Like elves and fairies in a ring,
> Enchanting all that you put in.

Music and a song, "Black spirits," &c.

[*Exit* Hecate.]

2. WITCH. By the pricking of my thumbs,
Something wicked this way comes.   45
        Open locks,
        Whoever knocks!

Enter Macbeth.

MACB.   How now, you secret, black, and midnight hags?
        What is't you do?

ALL.   A deed without a name.

MACB.   I conjure you by that which you profess   50
        (Howe'er you come to know it), answer me.
        Though you untie the winds and let them fight
        Against the churches; though the yesty waves
        Confound and swallow navigation up;
        Though bladed corn be lodg'd and trees blown down; 55
        Though castles topple on their warders' heads;
        Though palaces and pyramids do slope
        Their heads to their foundations; though the treasure
        Of nature's germens tumble all together,
        Even till destruction sicken — answer me   60
        To what I ask you.

1. WITCH.   Speak.

2. WITCH.   ,   Demand.

---

44 *pricking* Sudden pains in the body were regarded as signs of the approach of an evil person or a strange event.   50 *by . . . profess* the prophetic power which, as their words to him and Banquo had implied, they profess to have [K].   51 *Howe'er . . . it* no matter if your knowledge comes from infernal sources. He is determined to know "by the worst means the worst" (III.IV.135) [K].   52–61 *Though you . . . ask you* though the evil spells which you must use are so powerful as to bring utter ruin upon the whole earth, yet I will have you reveal the future to me [K].   52 *winds* Witches, particularly those of the North, were believed to control the weather.   53 *yesty* yeasty, foaming.   54 *Confound* destroy.   55 *bladed corn* If wheat in the blade is lodged (beaten down flat by wind and rain), the crop fails and famine ensues [K].   57 *slope* let fall.   58–9 *the treasure*

3. WITCH.   We'll answer.

1. WITCH. Say, if th' hadst rather hear it from our mouths
          Or from our masters.

MACB.   Call 'em! Let me see 'em.

1. WITCH. Pour in sow's blood, that hath eaten
          Her nine farrow; grease that's sweaten   65
          From the murderer's gibbet throw
          Into the flame.

ALL.   Come, high or low;
          Thyself and office deftly show!

                    Thunder. First Apparition, *an* Armed
                    Head.

MACB.   Tell me, thou unknown power —

1. WITCH.   He knows thy thought.
          Hear his speech, but say thou naught.   70

1. APPAR. Macbeth! Macbeth! Macbeth! Beware Macduff;
          Beware the Thane of Fife. Dismiss me. Enough.
                                        He descends.

MACB.   Whate'er thou art, for thy good caution thanks!
          Thou hast harp'd my fear aright. But one word more —

1. WITCH. He will not be commanded. Here's another,   75
          More potent than the first.

                    Thunder. Second Apparition, *a* Bloody
                    Child.

2. APPAR. Macbeth! Macbeth! Macbeth!

. . . *germens* the accumulated store of those elemental seeds or germs from which
everything in the future is to spring [K]. *germens* GLOBE; F¹: "Germaine."   60
sicken is satiated, and sickens at its own work [K].   63 *our masters* the great
powers of fate whom we serve. These are not to be confused with the imps or
familiars — Paddock, Graymalkin and Harpier [K].   65 *farrow* young pigs.
sweaten sweated. Perspiration was regarded as melted body fat. Here, that of a
murderer is used to make the fire flare up.   67 *high or low* wherever thou art,
whether in the upper or lower air, under the earth, or in hell [K].   68 *office*
function.   70 *Hear . . . naught* The powers which the Sisters have evoked are
so tremendous that they themselves stand in awe of them [K].   74 *harp'd . . .
aright* sounded it forth on the right string (expressed it truly) [K].

MACB.   Had I three ears, I'ld hear thee.

2. APPAR. Be bloody, bold, and resolute; laugh to scorn
          The pow'r of man, for none of woman born   80
          Shall harm Macbeth.   *Descends.*

MACB.   Then live, Macduff. What need I fear of thee?
          But yet I'll make assurance double sure
          And take a bond of fate. Thou shalt not live!
          That I may tell pale-hearted fear it lies   85
          And sleep in spite of thunder.

                    Thunder. Third Apparition, *a* Child
                    Crowned, *with a tree in his hand.*

                              What is this
          That rises like the issue of a king
          And wears upon his baby-brow the round
          And top of sovereignty?

ALL.   Listen, but speak not to't.

3. APPAR. Be lion-mettled, proud, and take no care   90
          Who chafes, who frets, or where conspirers are.
          Macbeth shall never vanquish'd be until
          Great Birnam Wood to high Dunsinane Hill
          Shall come against him.   *Descends.*

MACB.   That will never be.
          Who can impress the forest, bid the tree   95
          Unfix his earth-bound root? Sweet bodements, good!
          Rebellion's head rise never till the Wood
          Of Birnam rise, and our high-plac'd Macbeth
          Shall live the lease of nature, pay his breath
          To time and mortal custom. Yet my heart   100

---

84 *take a bond of fate* secure a guarantee from fate that she will keep her agree-
ment. By killing Macduff, Macbeth will put it out of Fate's power to harm him
unless Fate is ready to break two of her fixed laws: the law of birth and the law
of death: she must bring forward a man who was never born, and must bring
back a man (not a mere ghost) from the dead [K].   87 *like* in the shape of.
88–9 *round . . . top* the crown.   91 *chafes* is resentful.   95 *impress* conscript
forcibly.   96 *bodements* prophecies.   97 *Rebellion's head* THEOBALD; F¹: "Rebel-
lious dead." Those editors who would retain the F¹ reading argue that the refer-
ence is to Banquo's ghost.   *head* armed uprising.   99 *lease of nature* allotted time

Throbs to know one thing. Tell me, if your art
Can tell so much — shall Banquo's issue ever
Reign in this kingdom?

ALL.   Seek to know no more.

MACB.   I will be satisfied. Deny me this,
And an eternal curse fall on you! Let me know.   105
Why sinks that cauldron? and what noise is this?

                                    Hautboys.

1. WITCH. Show!

2. WITCH. Show!

3. WITCH. Show!

ALL.   Show his eyes, and grieve his heart!   110
Come like shadows, so depart!

                    A show of eight Kings, [*the eighth*]
                    with a glass in his hand, and Banquo
                    last.

MACB.   Thou art too like the spirit of Banquo. Down!
Thy crown does sear mine eyeballs. And thy hair,
Thou other gold-bound brow, is like the first.
A third is like the former. Filthy hags!   115
Why do you show me this? A fourth? Start, eyes!
What, will the line stretch out to th' crack of doom?
Another yet? A seventh? I'll see no more.
And yet the eighth appears, who bears a glass
Which shows me many more; and some I see   120
That twofold balls and treble sceptres carry.
Horrible sight! Now I see 'tis true;

---

of life.   100 *mortal custom* dying, common to all men.   104 *be satisfied* have full
information.   106 *noise* music.   111s.d. *show* a dumb show; an exhibition of actors
that do not speak [K].   116 *Start* bulge out.   119 *eighth* F³; F¹: "eight."   *glass*
a prospective or magic glass through which one can see the future.   121 *balls*
The "ball," "apple," or "orb" was one of the insignia of sovereignty. "Twofold"
refers to England and Scotland. "Treble" refers either to England, Scotland, and
Ireland, or more probably, to the title "King of Great Britain, France, and Ireland,"
assumed by James I in 1604. Banquo was the mythical ancestor of the Stuarts, of
whom James was the first to rule in England [K].

For the blood-bolter'd Banquo smiles upon me
And points at them for his. [*Apparitions vanish.*] What?
   Is this so?

1. WITCH. Ay, sir, all this is so. But why   125
   Stands Macbeth thus amazedly?
   Come, sisters, cheer we up his sprites
   And show the best of our delights.
   I'll charm the air to give a sound
   While you perform your antic round,   130
   That this great king may kindly say
   Our duties did his welcome pay.

          Music. The Witches *dance, and vanish.*

MACB. Where are they? Gone? Let this pernicious hour
   Stand aye accursed in the calendar!
   Come in, without there!

          Enter Lennox.

LEN.   What's your Grace's will?   135

MACB. Saw you the Weird Sisters?

LEN.   No, my lord.

MACB. Came they not by you?

LEN.   No indeed, my lord.

MACB. Infected be the air whereon they ride,
   And damn'd all those that trust them! I did hear
   The galloping of horse. Who was't came by?   140

LEN.   'Tis two or three, my lord, that bring you word
   Macduff is fled to England.

MACB.   Fled to England?

LEN.   Ay, my good lord.

---

123 *blood-bolter'd* with his hair matted with blood.   126 *amazedly* in a trance.
127 *sprites* spirits.   130 *antic round* fantastic dance.   136 *Weird* (F¹: "weyward").
139 *damn'd* Thus Macbeth, by implication, curses himself, for he trusts the Weird
Sisters to the very end [K].   144 *anticipat'st* forestallest.   145–6 *The flighty . . .
with it* every purpose is fleeting and will never be fulfilled unless it is accompanied
by the act proposed unless it is fulfilled as soon as formed [K].   147 *firstlings*

MACB.   [*aside*] Time, thou anticipat'st my dread exploits.
The flighty purpose never is o'ertook   145
Unless the deed go with it. From this moment
The very firstlings of my heart shall be
The firstlings of my hand. And even now,
To crown my thoughts with acts, be it thought and done!
The castle of Macduff I will surprise,   150
Seize upon Fife, give to the edge o' th' sword
His wife, his babes, and all unfortunate souls
That trace him in his line. No boasting like a fool!
This deed I'll do before this purpose cool.
But no more sights! — Where are these gentlemen?   155
Come, bring me where they are.   *Exeunt.*

◇◇◇◇◇◇◇◇◇◇◇◇◇◇◇

SCENE II. [*Fife.* Macduff's *Castle.*]

Enter Macduff's Wife, *her* Son, *and* Ross.

WIFE.   What had he done to make him fly the land?

ROSS.   You must have patience, madam.

WIFE.   He had none.
His flight was madness. When our actions do not,
Our fears do make us traitors.

ROSS.   You know not
Whether it was his wisdom or his fear.   5

WIFE.   Wisdom? To leave his wife, to leave his babes,
His mansion, and his titles, in a place
From whence himself does fly? He loves us not,
He wants the natural touch. For the poor wren,

---

first born; the first purposes his heart conceives.   153 *trace . . . line* follow him
as his descendants.
     IV.II. 2 *patience* self-control.   3–4 *When . . . traitors* Macduff had done
nothing treasonable. Yet fear had made him flee to the English court, and this
action had made him a traitor in fact [K].   7 *titles* possessions.   9 *natural touch*
natural trait which prompts all creatures to fight in defence of their young [K].

(The most diminutive of birds) will fight,   10
Her young ones in her nest, against the owl.
All is the fear, and nothing is the love,
  As little is the wisdom, where the flight
So runs against all reason.

ROSS.   My dearest coz,
I pray you school yourself. But for your husband,   15
He is noble, wise, judicious, and best knows
The fits o' th' season. I dare not speak much further;
But cruel are the times, when we are traitors
And do not know ourselves; when we hold rumour
From what we fear, yet know not what we fear,   20
But float upon a wild and violent sea
Each way and none. I take my leave of you.
Shall not be long but I'll be here again.
Things at the worst will cease, or else climb upward
To what they were before. — My pretty cousin,   25
Blessing upon you!

WIFE.   Father'd he is, and yet he's fatherless.

ROSS.   I am so much a fool, should I stay longer,
It would be my disgrace and your discomfort.
I take my leave at once.   *Exit.*

WIFE.   Sirrah, your father's dead;   30
And what will you do now? How will you live?

SON.   As birds do, mother.

WIFE.   What, with worms and flies?

SON.   With what I get, I mean; and so do they.

WIFE.   Poor bird! thou'dst never fear the net nor lime,
The pitfall nor the gin.   35

---

14 *coz* cousin, kinswoman.   15 *school* control. *for* as for.   17 *fits o' th' season*
sudden changes and disorders of these times.   18–19 *when we . . . ourselves*
when we are, in the King's eyes, traitors, yet do not know ourselves to be such,
are not conscious of having committed treason [K].   19–22 *when we hold . . .
none* when every rumour of danger is credited by us because of our fears, and yet
we do not really know what there is to be afraid of, since we are not conscious of
having committed any offence. Thus we are like a drifting hulk at sea, that is

SON.   Why should I, mother? Poor birds they are not set for.
       My father is not dead, for all your saying.

WIFE. Yes, he is dead. How wilt thou do for a father?

SON.   Nay, how will you do for a husband?

WIFE. Why, I can buy me twenty at any market.   40

SON.   Then you'll buy 'em to sell again.

WIFE. Thou speak'st with all thy wit; and yet, i' faith,
       With wit enough for thee.

SON.   Was my father a traitor, mother?

WIFE. Ay, that he was!   45

SON.   What is a traitor?

WIFE. Why, one that swears, and lies.

SON.   And be all traitors that do so?

WIFE. Every one that does so is a traitor and must be hang'd.

SON.   And must they all be hang'd that swear and lie?   50

WIFE. Every one.

SON.   Who must hang them?

WIFE. Why, the honest men.

SON.   Then the liars and swearers are fools; for there are liars
       and swearers enow to beat the honest men and hang up   55
       them.

WIFE. Now God help thee, poor monkey! But how wilt thou
       do for a father?

SON.   If he were dead, you'ld weep for him. If you would not,
       it were a good sign that I should quickly have a new   60
       father.

---

tossed about in every direction by shifting winds, but makes no progress in any
direction [K].   22 *none* WILSON; F¹: "moue."   24 *climb upward* improve.   29 *It
. . . discomfort* because I would weep, which is disgraceful in a man.   34 *lime*
birdlime, a sticky substance daubed on twigs to catch birds [K].   35 *pitfall* trap.
gin snare.   42-3 *Thou speak'st . . . thee* what you say is childish, for you have
but a child's wisdom, even when you use all of it — and yet, for a child, your wit
is well enough [K].   55 *enow* enough.

WIFE.   Poor prattler, how thou talk'st!

Enter a Messenger.

MESS.   Bless you, fair dame! I am not to you known,
Though in your state of honour I am perfect.
I doubt some danger does approach you nearly.   65
If you will take a homely man's advice,
Be not found here. Hence with your little ones!
To fright you thus methinks I am too savage;
To do worse to you were fell cruelty,
Which is too nigh your person. Heaven preserve you!   70
I dare abide no longer.   *Exit.*

WIFE.   Whither should I fly?
I have done no harm. But I remember now
I am in this earthly world, where to do harm
Is often laudable, to do good sometime
Accounted dangerous folly. Why then, alas,   75
Do I put up that womanly defence
To say I have done no harm? — What are these faces?

Enter Murderers.

MUR.   Where is your husband?

WIFE.   I hope, in no place so unsanctified
Where such as thou mayst find him.

MUR.   He's a traitor.   80

SON.   Thou liest, thou shag-ear'd villain!

MUR.   What, you egg!

                                        [*Stabs him.*]

SON.   Young fry of treachery!

---

64 *in your state . . . perfect* I am fully informed as to your honourable condition;
I know you well, honoured lady [K]   65 *doubt* fear.   66 *homely* simple, not a
noble.   69–70 *To do worse . . . person* not to warn you would be to do you
greater injury, to expose you to the cruelty which awaits you. *fell* fierce.   74
sometime sometimes.   81 *shag-ear'd* The long shaggy hair falling over the ruffian's
ears reminds the boy of a dog's ears [K]. This is the F¹ reading; some editors prefer
"shag-hair'd." *egg* unhatched chick, i.e. boy   82 *fry* spawn.
      IV.III. 3 *mortal* deadly.   4 *Bestride . . . birthdom* fight in defence of our

SON.   He has kill'd me, mother.
        Run away, I pray you!   [*Dies.*]

                        Exit [Wife], *crying* "Murder!" [*and
                        pursued by the* Murderers].

◇◇◇◇◇◇◇◇◇◇◇◇◇◇◇

        SCENE III.
        [*England. Before* King Edward's *Palace.*]

        Enter Malcolm *and* Macduff.

MAL.   Let us seek out some desolate shade, and there
        Weep our sad bosoms empty.

MACD.   Let us rather
        Hold fast the mortal sword and, like good men,
        Bestride our downfall'n birthdom. Each new morn
        New widows howl, new orphans cry, new sorrows   5
        Strike heaven on the face, that it resounds
        As if it felt with Scotland and yell'd out
        Like syllable of dolour.

MAL.   What I believe, I'll wail;
        What know, believe; and what I can redress,
        As I shall find the time to friend, I will.   10
        What you have spoke, it may be so perchance.
        This tyrant, whose sole name blisters our tongues,
        Was once thought honest; you have lov'd him well;
        He hath not touch'd you yet. I am young; but something
        You may deserve of him through me, and wisdom   15
        To offer up a weak, poor, innocent lamb

---

prostrate native land. The figure is from the old hand-to-hand combats, where it
was common for a man to bestride a fallen comrade to protect him in a melee
[K].   8 *Like . . . dolour* similar cries of pain.   10 *time to friend* opportunity to
be favourable.   12 *sole* mere.   13 *honest* honourable.   14–17 *I am young . . .
god* Though I am young and inexperienced, I cannot help seeing that you may be
trying to entrap me in order to maintain yourself in Macbeth's favour [K].   15
deserve THEOBALD; F¹: "discerne."   *through me* by betraying me.

       T' appease an angry god.

MACD.   I am not treacherous.

MAL.   But Macbeth is.
A good and virtuous nature may recoil
In an imperial charge. But I shall crave your pardon.   20
That which you are, my thoughts cannot transpose.
Angels are bright still, though the brightest fell.
Though all things foul would wear the brows of grace,
Yet grace must still look so.

MACD.   I have lost my hopes.

MAL.   Perchance even there where I did find my doubts.   25
Why in that rawness left you wife and child,
Those precious motives, those strong knots of love,
Without leave-taking? I pray you,
Let not my jealousies be your dishonours,
But mine own safeties. You may be rightly just,   30
Whatever I shall think.

MACD.   Bleed, bleed, poor country!
Great tyranny, lay thou thy basis sure,
For goodness dare not check thee! Wear thou thy wrongs;
The title is affeer'd! Fare thee well, lord.
I would not be the villain that thou think'st   35
For the whole space that's in the tyrant's grasp
And the rich East to boot.

MAL.   Be not offended.
I speak not as in absolute fear of you.
I think our country sinks beneath the yoke,
It weeps, it bleeds, and each new day a gash   40

19–20 *recoil . . . charge* give way under pressure from a monarch. The figure is either that of retiring before the onslaught ("charge") of a superior force, or that of a cannon which recoils when the charge (or load) is too great [K].   21 *transpose* transform. If Macduff is innocent of treachery, Malcolm's suspicions cannot make him guilty.   22 *brightest* Lucifer.   23 *would* should strive to. *brows of grace* face or appearance of virtue.   24 *so* like herself, virtuous.   25 *Perchance . . . doubts* perhaps what has made you lose your hopes is the very circumstance that has made me suspicious of you, your leaving your family in Macbeth's power, as you would hardly have done if you were his enemy [K].   26 *rawness* unprotected condition.   27 *motives* incentives to action.   29–30 *Let not . . . safeties* do not

Is added to her wounds. I think withal
There would be hands uplifted in my right:
And here from gracious England have I offer
Of goodly thousands. But, for all this,
When I shall tread upon the tyrant's head   45
Or wear it on my sword, yet my poor country
Shall have more vices than it had before,
More suffer and more sundry ways than ever,
By him that shall succeed.

MACD.   What should he be?

MAL.   It is myself I mean; in whom I know   50
All the particulars of vice so grafted
That, when they shall be open'd, black Macbeth
Will seem as pure as snow, and the poor state
Esteem him as a lamb, being compar'd
With my confineless harms.

MACD.   Not in the legions   55
Of horrid hell can come a devil more damn'd
In evils to top Macbeth.

MAL.   I grant him bloody,
Luxurious, avaricious, false, deceitful,
Sudden, malicious, smacking of every sin
That has a name. But there's no bottom, none,   60
In my voluptuousness. Your wives, your daughters,
Your matrons, and your maids could not fill up
The cistern of my lust; and my desire
All continent impediments would o'erbear
That did oppose my will. Better Macbeth   65

---

regard my suspicions as meant to dishonour you, but rather as proceeding from
a due regard for my own safety [K].   32 *basis* foundation.   33 *check* call to
account.   34 *title is affeer'd* legal right is affirmed.   41 *withal* besides.   43
England the English King.   51 *particulars* varieties.   *grafted* engrafted, im-
planted. The figure implies that these faults are so thoroughly incorporated in
Malcolm that they have become a part of his very being [K].   52 *open'd* brought
to light (as a bud opens).   55 *confineless harms* unlimited injuries.   57 *top* sur-
pass.   58 *Luxurious* lecherous.   59 *Sudden* violent.   61 *voluptuousness* lust.
63 *cistern* tank.   64 *continent* restraining.   *o'erbear* overpower.   65 *will* desire,
lust.

Than such an one to reign.

MACD.   Boundless intemperance
In nature is a tyranny. It hath been
Th' untimely emptying of the happy throne
And fall of many kings. But fear not yet
To take upon you what is yours. You may   70
Convey your pleasures in a spacious plenty,
And yet seem cold — the time you may so hoodwink.
We have willing dames enough. There cannot be
That vulture in you to devour so many
As will to greatness dedicate themselves,   75
Finding it so inclin'd.

MAL.   With this there grows
In my most ill-compos'd affection such
A stanchless avarice that, were I King,
I should cut off the nobles for their lands,
Desire his jewels, and this other's house,   80
And my more-having would be as a sauce
To make me hunger more, that I should forge
Quarrels unjust against the good and loyal,
Destroying them for wealth.

MACD.   This avarice
Sticks deeper, grows with more pernicious root   85
Than summer-seeming lust; and it hath been
The sword of our slain kings. Yet do not fear.
Scotland hath foisons to fill up your will
Of your mere own. All these are portable,
With other graces weigh'd.   90

66–7 *Boundless . . . tyranny* boundless incontinence is a tyranny in a man's nature, for it usurps absolute sway over all his other qualities [K].   71 *Convey*
manage secretly.   72 *cold* chaste. *time* the people. *hoodwink* delude.   74
vulture ravenous appetite.   75 *dedicate* offer up.   76 *Finding* if they find.
it greatness, the King.   77 *ill-compos'd affection* character made up of evil
elements.   78 *stanchless* insatiable.   81 *more-having* increase in wealth.   82
forge devise falsely.   85 *Sticks deeper* is more deeply rooted.   86 *summer-
seeming* befitting only the summertime of life, the warm and vigorous age, and
therefore not lasting so long as avarice [K].   87 *sword* killer.   88–9 *foisons . . .
mere own* riches (foisons) of your own enough to satisfy your greed (will).   89
portable endurable.   90 *With . . . weigh'd* balanced against your other virtues.

MAL.   But I have none. The king-becoming graces,
        As justice, verity, temp'rance, stableness,
        Bounty, perseverance, mercy, lowliness,
        Devotion, patience, courage, fortitude,
        I have no relish of them, but abound   95
        In the division of each several crime,
        Acting it many ways. Nay, had I pow'r, I should
        Pour the sweet milk of concord into hell,
        Uproar the universal peace, confound
        All unity on earth.

MACD.   O Scotland, Scotland!   100

MAL.   If such a one be fit to govern, speak.
        I am as I have spoken.

MACD.   Fit to govern?
        No, not to live. O nation miserable,
        With an untitled tyrant bloody-scept'red,
        When shalt thou see thy wholesome days again,   105
        Since that the truest issue of thy throne
        By his own interdiction stands accurs'd
        And does blaspheme his breed? Thy royal father
        Was a most sainted king; the queen that bore thee,
        Oft'ner upon her knees than on her feet,   110
        Died every day she liv'd. Fare thee well!
        These evils thou repeat'st upon thyself
        Have banish'd me from Scotland. O my breast,
        Thy hope ends here!

MAL.   Macduff, this noble passion,   114

91 *graces* virtues.   92 *temp'rance* self-control.   95 *relish of* taste for.   95–6 *abound . . . crime* in my actions I am abundantly guilty of every possible form of each sin [K].   99 *Uproar* change to tumultuous strife [K].   104 *untitled* without legal claim.   107 *interdiction* (a) curse (b) legal restriction placed upon one incapable of managing his own affairs.   107 *accurs'd* F²; F¹: "accust." Some editors read "accus'd."   108 *does . . . breed* slanders his parents by implying that they could naturally produce such a monster [K].   111 *Died . . . liv'd* referring to the penances and religious exercises by which she "died to the world." The phrase is a reminiscence of St Paul's "I died daily" (1 CORINTHIANS, XV, 31) [K].   114 *passion* emotion.

Child of integrity, hath from my soul   115
Wip'd the black scruples, reconcil'd my thoughts
To thy good truth and honour. Devilish Macbeth
By many of these trains hath sought to win me
Into his power; and modest wisdom plucks me
From over-credulous haste; but God above   120
Deal between thee and me! for even now
I put myself to thy direction and
Unspeak mine own detraction, here abjure
The taints and blames I laid upon myself
For strangers to my nature. I am yet   125
Unknown to woman, never was forsworn,
Scarcely have coveted what was mine own,
At no time broke my faith, would not betray
The devil to his fellow, and delight
No less in truth than life. My first false speaking 130
Was this upon myself. What I am truly,
Is thine and my poor country's to command.
Whither indeed, before thy here-approach,
Old Siward with ten thousand warlike men
Already at a point was setting forth.   135
Now we'll together; and the chance of goodness
Be like our warranted quarrel! Why are you silent?

MACD.   Such welcome and unwelcome things at once
'Tis hard to reconcile.

Enter a Doctor.

MAL.   Well, more anon. Comes the King forth, I pray you?   140

DOCT.   Ay, sir. There are a crew of wretched souls

---

115 *Child* product.   116 *scruples* doubts.   116–17 *reconcil'd . . . honour* brought
my opinion of you into accord with your real character as a loyal and honourable
man [K].   118 *trains* stratagems.   *win* entice.   119 *modest wisdom* prudent
caution.   122 *direction* guidance.   124 *taints* stains.   125 *For* as.   131 *upon*
against.   133 *thy* F²; F¹: "they."   135 *at a point* fully prepared.   136–7 *chance
. . . quarrel* may our chance of success be as good as our cause is just [K].   142
stay await.   *cure* To Shakespeare's contemporaries the most familiar fact about
King Edward was the legend that he was the first English king to cure scrofula
by touching [K]. The good use of the supernatural here is contrasted to its evil
use by the Weird Sisters.   142–3 *convinces . . . art* baffles the utmost efforts of
medical science [K].   145 *presently* instantly.   *amend* recover.   146 *the evil* the

That stay his cure. Their malady convinces
The great assay of art; but at his touch,
Such sanctity hath heaven given his hand,
They presently amend.

MAL.   I thank you, doctor.   145

Exit [Doctor].

MACD.   What's the disease he means?

MAL.   'Tis call'd the evil:
A most miraculous work in this good king,
Which often since my here-remain in England
I have seen him do. How he solicits heaven
Himself best knows; but strangely-visited people,   150
All swol'n and ulcerous, pitiful to the eye,
The mere despair of surgery, he cures,
Hanging a golden stamp about their necks,
Put on with holy prayers; and 'tis spoken,
To the succeeding royalty he leaves   155
The healing benediction. With this strange virtue,
He hath a heavenly gift of prophecy,
And sundry blessings hang about his throne
That speak him full of grace.

Enter Ross.

MACD.   See who comes here.

MAL.   My countryman; but yet I know him not.   160

MACD.   My ever gentle cousin, welcome hither.

MAL.   I know him now. Good God betimes remove

---

king's evil, scrofula.   148 *here-remain* sojourn here (POPE; F¹: "heere remaine").
149 *solicits heaven* prays.   150 *strangely-visited* afflicted with horrible disease
(POPE; F¹: "strangely visited").   152 *mere* utter.   153 *stamp* coin (which the King
gave to those he touched).   155 *succeeding royalty* kings descended from him.
King James I, although at first reluctant to do so, had continued the practice of
touching scrofula victims upon the urging of his ministers. This passage is thought
to have been designed as a compliment to him.   159 *grace* holiness.   160 *My*
countryman . . . not Malcolm knows that Ross is a Scot from his costume, but
he fails to recognize him until he speaks. This indicates that Malcolm has been
long absent from Scotland [K].   *not* (F¹: "nor").   162 *betimes* speedily.

The means that makes us strangers!

ROSS.   Sir, amen.

MACD.   Stands Scotland where it did?

ROSS.   Alas, poor country,
Almost afraid to know itself! It cannot   165
Be call'd our mother, but our grave; where nothing,
But who knows nothing, is once seen to smile;
Where sighs and groans, and shrieks that rent the air,
Are made, not mark'd; where violent sorrow seems
A modern ecstasy. The dead man's knell   170
Is there scarce ask'd for who; and good men's lives
Expire before the flowers in their caps,
Dying or ere they sicken.

MACD.   O, relation
Too nice, and yet too true!

MAL.   What's the newest grief?

ROSS.   That of an hour's age doth hiss the speaker;   175
Each minute teems a new one.

MACD.   How does my wife?

ROSS.   Why, well.

MACD.   And all my children?

ROSS.   Well too.

MACD.   The tyrant has not batter'd at their peace?

ROSS.   No; they were well at peace when I did leave 'em.

MACD.   Be not a niggard of your speech. How goes't?   180

ROSS.   When I came hither to transport the tidings
Which I have heavily borne, there ran a rumour

---

163 *means . . . strangers* Macbeth, who is responsible for Malcolm's absence from
Scotland [K].   165 *know itself* look its own misfortunes in the face [K].   167 *who*
one who.   168 *rent* rend.   169 *mark'd* noticed.   170 *modern ecstasy* common-
place emotion.   171 *who* whom.   173 *Dying or ere they sicken* dying before they
sicken — by violence, not a natural death [K].   *relation* recital.   174 *nice* minutely
accurate.   175 *That . . . speaker* the report of any dreadful thing that happened
but an hour ago causes the teller to be hissed for his stale news, so much has
occurred in the interim [K].   176 *teems* gives birth to.   182 *heavily* sadly.   183

Of many worthy fellows that were out;
Which was to my belief witness'd the rather
For that I saw the tyrant's power afoot.   185
Now is the time of help. Your eye in Scotland
Would create soldiers, make our women fight
To doff their dire distresses.

MAL.   Be't their comfort
We are coming thither. Gracious England hath
Lent us good Siward and ten thousand men.   190
An older and a better soldier none
That Christendom gives out.

ROSS.   Would I could answer
This comfort with the like! But I have words
That would be howl'd out in the desert air,
Where hearing should not latch them.

MACD.   What concern they? 195
The general cause? or is it a fee-grief
Due to some single breast?

ROSS.   No mind that's honest
But in it shares some woe, though the main part
Pertains to you alone.

MACD.   If it be mine,
Keep it not from me, quickly let me have it.   200

ROSS.   Let not your ears despise my tongue for ever,
Which shall possess them with the heaviest sound
That ever yet they heard.

MACD.   Humh! I guess at it.

ROSS.   Your castle is surpris'd; your wife and babes

---

out in the field, under arms.   185 *For that* because. *power* troops. *afoot*
mobilized.   188 *doff* put off.   189 *England* the English King.   192 *gives out*
proclaims.   194 *would* should.   195 *latch* catch.   196 *fee-grief* grief that is one
man's possession; a personal sorrow — one that belongs to him alone, as in fee
simple [K].   197 *Due* belonging. *honest* honourable.   202 *heaviest* saddest.
204 *surpris'd* seized.   206 *quarry* slaughtered bodies; literally, the whole amount
of game killed in a single hunt. The pun on "deer" and "dear" was so common
as not to shock the hearer [K].

	Savagely slaughter'd. To relate the manner,	205
	Were, on the quarry of these murder'd deer,	
	To add the death of you.	

MAL.   Merciful heaven!
What, man! Ne'er pull your hat upon your brows.
Give sorrow words. The grief that does not speak
Whispers the o'erfraught heart and bids it break.   210

MACD.   My children too?

ROSS.   Wife, children, servants, all
That could be found.

MACD.   And I must be from thence?
My wife kill'd too?

ROSS.   I have said.

MAL.   Be comforted.
Let's make us med'cines of our great revenge
To cure this deadly grief.   215

MACD.   He has no children. All my pretty ones?
Did you say all? O hell-kite! All?
What, all my pretty chickens and their dam
At one fell swoop?

MAL.   Dispute it like a man.

MACD.   I shall do so;   220
But I must also feel it as a man.
I cannot but remember such things were
That were most precious to me. Did heaven look on
And would not take their part? Sinful Macduff,
They were all struck for thee! Naught that I am,   225

---

210 *o'erfraught* overburdened.   216 *He has no children* The line has been variously interpreted: (a) Macbeth has none; if he had he could not have killed mine
[K] (b) Macbeth has none, and thus Macduff cannot take proper revenge against
him (c) Malcolm has no children and thus can have no comprehension of Macduff's
grief; this is the least likely interpretation.   217 *hell-kite* hellish bird of prey.
220 *Dispute it* resist it; withstand your grief [K].   225 *Naught* Wicked man.
226 *Not for . . . mine* they were slain because of Macduff's offences against Macbeth; but that is not quite all that Macduff has in mind. He thinks of their

Not for their own demerits, but for mine,
Fell slaughter on their souls. Heaven rest them now!

MAL.   Be this the whetstone of your sword. Let grief
Convert to anger; blunt not the heart, enrage it.

MACD.   O, I could play the woman with mine eyes   230
And braggart with my tongue! But, gentle heavens,
Cut short all intermission. Front to front
Bring thou this fiend of Scotland and myself.
Within my sword's length set him. If he scape,
Heaven forgive him too!

MAL.   This tune goes manly.   235
Come, go we to the King. Our power is ready;
Our lack is nothing but our leave. Macbeth
Is ripe for shaking, and the pow'rs above
Put on their instruments. Receive what cheer you may.
The night is long that never finds the day.   *Exeunt.*

murder as also a judgment sent from God upon his sins in general [K].   229
Convert change.   230 *play the woman* weep.   232 *intermission* delay, interval
between actions.   *Front to front* face to face.   235 *tune* ROWE; F¹: "time."   236
power forces.   237 *Our . . . leave* nothing remains to do except to take our leave
of King Edward and receive his permission to depart [K].   238 *ripe for shaking*
The figure is from ripe fruit which is ready to fall when the tree is shaken [K].
239 *Put on their instruments* (a) are urging us, their agents, to action [K] (b) arm
themselves.   *cheer* comfort.

Act Five

SCENE 1. [*Dunsinane*. Macbeth's *Castle*.]

Enter a Doctor of Physic *and a* Waiting Gentlewoman.

DOCT.   I have two nights watch'd with you, but can perceive no truth in your report. When was it she last walk'd?

GENT.   Since his Majesty went into the field I have seen her rise from her bed, throw her nightgown upon her, unlock her closet, take forth paper, fold it, write upon't, read it,   5
afterwards seal it, and again return to bed; yet all this while in a most fast sleep.

DOCT.   A great perturbation in nature, to receive at once the benefit of sleep and do the effects of watching! In this slumb'ry agitation, besides her walking and other actual   10
performances, what (at any time) have you heard her say?

GENT.   That, sir, which I will not report after her.

DOCT.   You may to me, and 'tis most meet you should.

GENT.   Neither to you nor any one, having no witness to confirm   15
my speech.

Enter Lady [Macbeth], *with a taper.*

Lo you, here she comes! This is her very guise, and, upon my life, fast asleep! Observe her; stand close.

V.I.   3 *went into the field* set out with his army.   4 *nightgown* dressing gown.
5 *closet* chest or desk.   9 *do . . . watching* do the acts appropriate to a waking
condition.   10 *slumb'ry agitation* disturbed action while asleep, sleepwalking.
actual exhibited in deeds.   14 *meet* fitting, proper.   17 *her very guise* the exact

DOCT.   How came she by that light?

GENT.   Why, it stood by her. She has light by her continually.   20
'Tis her command.

DOCT.   You see her eyes are open.

GENT.   Ay; but their sense are shut.

DOCT.   What is it she does now? Look how she rubs her hands.

GENT.   It is an accustom'd action with her, to seem thus wash-   25
ing her hands. I have known her continue in this a
quarter of an hour.

LADY.   Yet here's a spot.

DOCT.   Hark, she speaks! I will set down what comes from her,
to satisfy my remembrance the more strongly.   30

LADY.   Out, damned spot! out, I say! One; two. Why then 'tis
time to do't. Hell is murky. Fie, my lord, fie! a soldier,
and afeard? What need we fear who knows it, when none
can call our pow'r to accompt? Yet who would have
thought the old man to have had so much blood in him?   35

DOCT.   Do you mark that?

LADY.   The Thane of Fife had a wife. Where is she now? What,
will these hands ne'er be clean? No more o' that, my
lord, no more o' that! You mar all with this starting.

DOCT.   Go to, go to! You have known what you should not.   40

GENT.   She has spoke what she should not, I am sure of that.
Heaven knows what she has known.

LADY.   Here's the smell of the blood still. All the perfumes of
Arabia will not sweeten this little hand. Oh, oh, oh!

DOCT.   What a sigh is there! The heart is sorely charg'd.   45

---

way in which I have described her appearance [K].   18 *close* hidden.   23 *sense*
sight. *are* F¹; ROWE, K: "is."   30 *satisfy* confirm.   32 *murky* dark.   34 *accompt*
account.   39 *starting* startled movements — as at the Banquet scene.   45 *charg'd*
burdened.

GENT.   I would not have such a heart in my bosom for the dignity of the whole body.

DOCT.   Well, well, well.

GENT.   Pray God it be, sir.

DOCT.   This disease is beyond my practice. Yet I have known   50
those which have walk'd in their sleep who have died
holily in their beds.

LADY.   Wash your hands, put on your nightgown, look not so
pale! I tell you yet again, Banquo's buried. He can not
come out on's grave.   55

DOCT.   Even so?

LADY.   To bed, to bed! There's knocking at the gate. Come,
come, come, come, give me your hand! What's done
cannot be undone. To bed, to bed, to bed!   *Exit.*

DOCT.   Will she go now to bed?   60

GENT.   Directly.

DOCT.   Foul whisp'rings are abroad. Unnatural deeds
Do breed unnatural troubles. Infected minds
To their deaf pillows will discharge their secrets.
More needs she the divine than the physician.   65
God, God forgive us all! Look after her;
Remove from her the means of all annoyance,
And still keep eyes upon her. So good night.
My mind she has mated, and amaz'd my sight.
I think, but dare not speak.

GENT.   Good night, good doctor.

                                               Exeunt.

---

50 *practice* ability to cure.   63 *Infected* diseased because of guilt [K].   64 *discharge* unload, reveal.   67 *annoyance* injury (to herself, suicide).   68 *still* always. 69 *mated* paralyzed, confounded.

V.II. 1 pow'r *army*.   2 *uncle* In Holinshed, Malcolm's mother is Earl Siward's daughter [K].   3 *dear causes* heartfelt grounds for accusation.   4–5 *Would . . . man* would rouse to action even a paralytic and make him join the rest in the fierce and bloody onset [K].   6 *well* probably.   8 *file* list.   10 *unrough* smooth-faced, beardless.   11 *Protest . . . manhood* declare (by going to war) that they

◇◇◇◇◇◇◇◇◇◇◇◇◇◇◇◇◇

SCENE II. [*The country near Dunsinane.*]

Drum and Colours. Enter Menteith, Caithness, Angus,
    Lennox, Soldiers.

MENT.   The English pow'r is near, led on by Malcolm,
His uncle Siward, and the good Macduff.
Revenges burn in them; for their dear causes
Would to the bleeding and the grim alarm
Excite the mortified man.

ANG.   Near Birnam Wood   5
Shall we well meet them; that way are they coming.

CAITH.   Who knows if Donalbain be with his brother?

LEN.   For certain, sir, he is not. I have a file
Of all the gentry. There is Siward's son
And many unrough youths that even now   10
Protest their first of manhood.

MENT.   What does the tyrant?

CAITH.   Great Dunsinane he strongly fortifies.
Some say he's mad; others, that lesser hate him,
Do call it valiant fury; but for certain
He cannot buckle his distemper'd cause   15
Within the belt of rule.

ANG.   Now does he feel
His secret murders sticking on his hands.
Now minutely revolts upbraid his faith-breach.
Those he commands move only in command,

---

are now first acting a man's part [K].   14 *valiant fury* the frenzy of desperate
valour [K].   15–16 *He cannot . . . rule* the cause for which he fights is so bad
that he cannot restrain himself within the bounds of self-control in supporting it
[K].   *distemper'd* diseased. The figure is of a dropsical person, swollen beyond the
limits of a normal girdle [K].   *rule* self-control.   17 *sticking on his hands* A
graphic figure, suggesting the viscous quality of coagulated blood, and reminding
us of Lady Macbeth's effort to wash it from her hands [K].   18 *minutely* every
minute.   *revolts . . . faith-breach* rebellions rebuke him for his own treason.

Nothing in love. Now does he feel his title   20
Hang loose about him, like a giant's robe
Upon a dwarfish thief.

MENT.   Who then shall blame
His pester'd senses to recoil and start,
When all that is within him does condemn
Itself for being there?

CAITH.   Well, march we on   25
To give obedience where 'tis truly ow'd.
Meet we the med'cine of the sickly weal;
And with him pour we in our country's purge
Each drop of us.

LEN.   Or so much as it needs
To dew the sovereign flower and drown the weeds.   30
Make we our march towards Birnam.

                                    Exeunt, marching.

❖❖❖❖❖❖❖❖❖❖❖❖❖❖

SCENE III.
[*Dunsinane. A room in the Castle.*]

Enter Macbeth, Doctor, *and* Attendants.

MACB.   Bring me no more reports. Let them fly all!
Till Birnam Wood remove to Dunsinane,
I cannot taint with fear. What's the boy Malcolm?
Was he not born of woman? The spirits that know
All mortal consequences have pronounc'd me thus: 5

---

19 *in* because of.   23 *pester'd senses* tormented mind.   24–5 *When all . . . there*
for, when he looks into his mind, he sees nothing but consciousness of guilt [K].
27 *med'cine . . . weal* the physician who will cure the commonwealth, Malcolm.
28 *purge* cleansing draught, physic.   29–30 *Or so . . . weeds* their blood is to
"bedew" or "water" the flower of legitimate sovereignty (Malcolm) and make it
thrive, and at the same time is to "drown out" the weeds of usurpation and
tyranny [K].

V.III. 3 *taint* become tainted.   5 *mortal consequences* not results; but simply
future events in human life [K].

"Fear not, Macbeth. No man that's born of woman
Shall e'er have power upon thee." Then fly, false thanes,
And mingle with the English epicures.
The mind I sway by and the heart I bear
Shall never sag with doubt nor shake with fear.   10

Enter Servant.

The devil damn thee black, thou cream-fac'd loon!
Where got'st thou that goose look?

SERV.   There is ten thousand —

MACB.   Geese, villain?

SERV.   Soldiers, sir.

MACB.   Go prick thy face and over-red thy fear,
Thou lily-liver'd boy. What soldiers, patch?   15
Death of thy soul! Those linen cheeks of thine
Are counsellors to fear. What soldiers, wheyface?

SERV.   The English force, so please you.

MACB.   Take thy face hence.   [*Exit Servant.*]
                    Seyton! — I am sick at heart,
When I behold — Seyton, I say! — This push   20
Will cheer me ever, or disseat me now.
I have liv'd long enough. My way of life
Is fall'n into the sere, the yellow leaf;
And that which should accompany old age,
As honour, love, obedience, troops of friends,   25
I must not look to have; but, in their stead,

---

8 *epicures* The English were regarded by the Scots as living in luxurious plenty
[K].   9 *I sway by* which governs my actions.   11 *damn thee black* Damned souls
were regarded as coloured black, the colour of the devil himself.   15 *lily-liver'd*
white-livered, cowardly. Fear was supposed to be caused by lack of red blood in
the liver [K].   *patch* fool.   16 *linen* pale as white linen.   17 *counsellors to*
inciters of others to.   20 *push* final effort, attack.   21 *Will cheer . . . now*
will either give me peace and happiness for ever or dethrone me instantly and
once for all [K].   23 *sere . . . leaf* the autumn season.

Curses not loud but deep, mouth-honour, breath,
Which the poor heart would fain deny, and dare not.
Seyton!

Enter Seyton.

SEY.   What's your gracious pleasure?

MACB.   What news more?   30

SEY.   All is confirm'd, my lord, which was reported.

MACB.   I'll fight, till from my bones my flesh be hack'd.
Give me my armour.

SEY.   'Tis not needed yet.

MACB.   I'll put it on.
Send out moe horses, skirr the country round;   35
Hang those that talk of fear. Give me mine armour.
How does your patient, doctor?

DOCT.   Not so sick, my lord,
As she is troubled with thick-coming fancies
That keep her from her rest.

MACB.   Cure her of that!
Canst thou not minister to a mind diseas'd,   40
Pluck from the memory a rooted sorrow,
Raze out the written troubles of the brain,
And with some sweet oblivious antidote
Cleanse the stuff'd bosom of that perilous stuff
Which weighs upon the heart?

DOCT.   Therein the patient   45
Must minister to himself.

MACB.   Throw physic to the dogs, I'll none of it! —

---

27 *mouth-honour* All that Macbeth can expect is homage in words, which the
heart of the liegeman does not prompt, but would refuse if it dared [K].   35 *moe*
more. *skirr* scour.   39 *Cure her* F²; F¹: "cure."   42 *Raze out* erase.   43 *oblivious
antidote* opiate, medicine to cause forgetfulness.   44 *stuff'd* clogged, choked with
fullness.   50 *dispatch* make haste.   50-1 *cast . . . land* make a diagnosis of the
disease from which Scotland is suffering. A medical figure from examination of a

Come, put mine armour on. Give me my staff. —
Seyton, send out. — Doctor, the thanes fly from me. —
Come, sir, dispatch. — If thou couldst, doctor, cast   50
The water of my land, find her disease,
And purge it to a sound and pristine health,
I would applaud thee to the very echo,
That should applaud again. — Pull't off, I say. —
What rhubarb, senna, or what purgative drug,   55
Would scour these English hence? Hear'st thou of them?

DOCT.   Ay, my good lord. Your royal preparation
Makes us hear something.

MACB.   Bring it after me!
I will not be afraid of death and bane
Till Birnam Forest come to Dunsinane.   60

[Exeunt all but the Doctor.]

DOCT.   Were I from Dunsinane away and clear,
Profit again should hardly draw me here.   *Exit.*

❖❖❖❖❖❖❖❖❖❖❖❖❖❖❖❖

SCENE IV. [*Country near Birnam Wood.*]

Drum and Colours. Enter Malcolm, Siward, Macduff,
Siward's Son, Menteith, Caithness, Angus, [Lennox,
Ross,] *and* Soldiers, *marching.*

MAL.   Cousins, I hope the days are near at hand
That chambers will be safe.

MENT.   We doubt it nothing.

---

patient's urine [K].   52 *pristine* such as formerly existed (F²; F¹: "pristiue").
55 *senna* a purgative drug (F⁴; F¹: "Cyme").   56 *scour* purge, clear away.   59
bane destruction.

V.IV. 2 *chambers . . . safe* men will not have to worry about being murdered
in their bedrooms like Duncan. *nothing* not at all.

SIW.   What wood is this before us?

MENT.   The Wood of Birnam.

MAL.   Let every soldier hew him down a bough
            And bear't before him. Thereby shall we shadow   5
            The numbers of our host and make discovery
            Err in report of us.

SOLDIERS.   It shall be done.

SIW.   We learn no other but the confident tyrant
            Keeps still in Dunsinane and will endure
            Our setting down before't.

MAL.   'Tis his main hope;   10
            For where there is advantage to be given,
            Both more and less have given him the revolt;
            And none serve with him but constrained things,
            Whose hearts are absent too.

MACD.   Let our just censures
            Attend the true event, and put we on   15
            Industrious soldiership.

SIW.   The time approaches
            That will with due decision make us know
            What we shall say we have, and what we owe.
            Thoughts speculative their unsure hopes relàte,
            But certain issue strokes must arbitrate;   20
            Towards which advance the war.   *Exeunt, marching.*

4–5 *Let every . . . before him* This stratagem is a very old piece of popular fiction
and is widespread in folk tales [K].   5 *shadow* becloud, conceal.   6 *discovery*
reports by Macbeth's scouts.   10 *setting down* laying siege.   11 *advantage* opportunity.   12 *more and less* nobles and commoners.   13 *things* used contemptu-
ously for persons who, being constrained, have no will of their own and are
therefore mere instruments rather than men [K].   14–16 *Let . . . soldiership* let
our opinions, in order that they may be accurate, wait for the outcome, which is
sure to disclose the truth; and meantime let us use all our skill and energy in the
campaign [K].   19–20 *Thoughts . . . arbitrate* guesses can only reflect our own

◇◇◇◇◇◇◇◇◇◇◇◇◇◇◇◇◇

SCENE V. [*Dunsinane. Within the Castle.*]

Enter Macbeth, Seyton, *and* Soldiers, *with* Drum *and*
    Colours.

MACB.   Hang out our banners on the outward walls.
    The cry is still, "They come!" Our castle's strength
    Will laugh a siege to scorn. Here let them lie
    Till famine and the ague eat them up.
    Were they not forc'd with those that should be ours,   5
    We might have met them dareful, beard to beard,
    And beat them backward home.
                                    A cry within of women.
                        What is that noise?

SEY.   It is the cry of women, my good lord.   [*Exit.*]

MACB.   I have almost forgot the taste of fears.
    The time has been, my senses would have cool'd   10
    To hear a night-shriek, and my fell of hair
    Would at a dismal treatise rouse and stir
    As life were in't. I have supp'd full with horrors.
    Direness, familiar to my slaughterous thoughts,
    Cannot once start me.

                        [*Enter Seyton.*]

                        Wherefore was that cry?   15

SEY.   The Queen, my lord, is dead.

MACB.   She should have died hereafter;
    There would have been a time for such a word.
    To-morrow, and to-morrow, and to-morrow
    Creeps in this petty pace from day to day   20

---

hopes; it is only by fighting that we can learn how the battle will come out.
arbitrate decide.

    V.v. 2 *still* always.   3 *lie* are encamped.   4 *ague* pestilence.   5 *forc'd* reinforced.
6 *dareful* boldly.   9 *fears* objects or causes of fear [K].   10 *cool'd* felt the chill
of terror [K].   11 *fell of hair* hair on my skin.   12 *treatise* story.   13 *As* as if.
14 *Direness* horror.   15 *start* startle.   17 *She should . . . hereafter* she would
inevitably have died at some time (if she had not died now). Thus Macbeth hears
the news of his wife's death with complete apathy.

To the last syllable of recorded time;
And all our yesterdays have lighted fools
The way to dusty death. Out, out, brief candle!
Life's but a walking shadow, a poor player,
That struts and frets his hour upon the stage   25
And then is heard no more. It is a tale
Told by an idiot, full of sound and fury,
Signifying nothing.

Enter a Messenger.

Thou com'st to use thy tongue. Thy story quickly!

MESS.   Gracious my lord,   30
I should report that which I say I saw,
But know not how to do't.

MACB.   Well, say, sir!

MESS.   As I did stand my watch upon the hill,
I look'd toward Birnam, and anon methought
The wood began to move.

MACB.   Liar and slave!   35

MESS.   Let me endure your wrath if't be not so.
Within this three mile may you see it coming;
I say, a moving grove.

MACB.   If thou speak'st false,
Upon the next tree shalt thou hang alive,
Till famine cling thee. If thy speech be sooth,   40
I care not if thou dost for me as much.
I pull in resolution, and begin
To doubt th' equivocation of the fiend,

---

21 *recorded time* time, as opposed to eternity (in which there are no yesterdays
and no tomorrows) [K].   23 *brief* short-lived.   25 *struts and frets* shows Macbeth's contempt, not for the actor, but for human life. The player does not act
real life, he only imitates it; but after all, life itself is as poor a thing, as much
of a mockery of reality, as the player's art is a mockery of life; and both life and
the actor's art are pitifully transitory things [K].   39 *shalt* (F¹: "shall").   40 *cling*

That lies like truth. "Fear not, till Birnam Wood   45
Do come to Dunsinane!" and now a wood
Comes toward Dunsinane. Arm, arm, and out!
If this which he avouches does appear,
There is nor flying hence nor tarrying here.
I gin to be aweary of the sun,
And wish th' estate o' th' world were now undone.   50
Ring the alarum bell! Blow wind, come wrack,
At least we'll die with harness on our back!   *Exeunt.*

◆◇◆◇◆◇◆◇◆◇◆◇◆◇◆◇◆

S C E N E V I. [*Dunsinane. Before the Castle.*]

Drum and Colours. Enter Malcolm, Siward, Macduff,
and their Army, *with boughs.*

MAL.   Now near enough. Your leavy screens throw down
And show like those you are. You, worthy uncle,
Shall with my cousin, your right noble son,
Lead our first battle. Worthy Macduff and we
Shall take upon's what else remains to do,   5
According to our order.

SIW.   Fare you well.
Do we but find the tyrant's power to-night,
Let us be beaten if we cannot fight.

MACD.   Make all our trumpets speak, give them all breath,
Those clamorous harbingers of blood and death.
                              Exeunt. Alarums continued.

wither. *sooth* truth.   42 *pull in* rein in, check.   43 *To doubt . . . fiend* to
suspect that Satan has been cheating me by his regular device of ambiguous
prophecies [K].   48 *avouches* affirms.   49 *gin* begin.   50 *th' estate . . . undone*
the orderly universe reduced to chaos.   51 *wrack* ruin.   52 *harness* armour.
    V.VI. 1 *leavy* leafy.   2 *show* appear.   4 *battle* battalion.   6 *order* previous
arrangements.   7 *Do we* if we do.   *power* forces.

◇◇◇◇◇◇◇◇◇◇◇◇◇◇◇◇

SCENE VII. [*Another part of the field.*]

Enter Macbeth.

MACB.   They have tied me to a stake. I cannot fly,
But bear-like I must fight the course. What's he
That was not born of woman? Such a one
Am I to fear, or none.

Enter Young Siward.

Y. SIW.   What is thy name?

MACB.   Thou'lt be afraid to hear it.   5

Y. SIW.   No; though thou call'st thyself a hotter name
Than any is in hell.

MACB.   My name's Macbeth.

Y. SIW.   The devil himself could not pronounce a title
More hateful to mine ear.

MACB.   No, nor more fearful.

Y. SIW.   Thou liest, abhorred tyrant! With my sword   10
I'll prove the lie thou speak'st.

Fight, and Young Siward *slain.*

MACB.   Thou wast born of woman.
But swords I smile at, weapons laugh to scorn,
Brandish'd by man that's of a woman born.   *Exit.*

Alarums. Enter Macduff.

MACD.   That way the noise is. Tyrant, show thy face!
If thou beest slain and with no stroke of mine,   15
My wife and children's ghosts will haunt me still.

V.VII. 1 *tied . . . stake* A figure from bear-baiting, in which the bear was tied
to a post and attacked by dogs. Macbeth's castle is surrounded, so that he cannot
escape. He has made a sally (V.v.46), but has failed to break through the be-
siegers and has retired to his defences [K].   2 *course* one run at the bear by the
dogs.   16 *still* forever.   17 *kerns* Irish guerrilla soldiers, here used in the sense
of any mercenaries.   18 *staves* spears.   20 *undeeded* not honoured by any
martial deed.   21–2 *By this . . . bruited* this noise seems to proclaim one of

I cannot strike at wretched kerns, whose arms
Are hir'd to bear their staves. Either thou, Macbeth,
Or else my sword with an unbattered edge
I sheathe again undeeded. There thou shouldst be.   20
By this great clatter one of greatest note
Seems bruited. Let me find him, Fortune!
And more I beg not.   *Exit. Alarums.*

Enter Malcolm *and* Siward.

SIW.   This way, my lord. The castle's gently rend'red:
The tyrant's people on both sides do fight;   25
The noble thanes do bravely in the war;
The day almost itself professes yours,
And little is to do.

MAL.   We have met with foes
That strike beside us.

SIW.   Enter, sir, the castle.
                        Exeunt. Alarum.

◇◇◇◇◇◇◇◇◇◇◇◇◇◇◇◇◇◇

SCENE VIII. [*Another part of the field.*]

Enter Macbeth.

MACB.   Why should I play the Roman fool and die
On mine own sword? Whiles I see lives, the gashes
Do better upon them.

Enter Macduff.

MACD.   Turn, hellhound, turn!

MACB.   Of all men else I have avoided thee.

---

greatest station.   24 *gently rend'red* surrendered without defence.   26 *bravely*
splendidly.   27 *itself professes* declares itself.   29 *strike beside us* let their blows
fall by our sides without trying to hit us [K].

    V.VIII. 1 *play the Roman fool* commit suicide, as Roman officers often did when
faced with defeat.   2 *Whiles . . . lives* so long as I see any of the enemy
alive [K].

But get thee back! My soul is too much charg'd   5
With blood of thine already.

MACD.   I have no words;
My voice is in my sword, thou bloodier villain
Than terms can give thee out!   *Fight. Alarum.*

MACB.   Thou losest labour.
As easy mayst thou the intrenchant air
With thy keen sword impress as make me bleed.   10
Let fall thy blade on vulnerable crests.
I bear a charmed life, which must not yield
To one of woman born.

MACD.   Despair thy charm!
And let the angel whom thou still hast serv'd
Tell thee, Macduff was from his mother's womb   15
Untimely ripp'd.

MACB.   Accursed be that tongue that tells me so,
For it hath cow'd my better part of man!
And be these juggling fiends no more believ'd,
That palter with us in a double sense,   20
That keep the word of promise to our ear
And break it to our hope! I'll not fight with thee!

MACD.   Then yield thee, coward,
And live to be the show and gaze o' th' time!
We'll have thee, as our rarer monsters are,   25
Painted upon a pole, and underwrit
"Here may you see the tyrant."

MACB.   I will not yield,
To kiss the ground before young Malcolm's feet
And to be baited with the rabble's curse.
Though Birnam Wood be come to Dunsinane,   30

---

5 *charg'd* loaded, burdened.   8 *give thee out* name thee.   9 *intrenchant* incapable of being cut.   10 *impress* make an impression on.   11 *crests* heads.
13 *Despair thy charm* let thy charm be a ground for despair rather than for
confidence.   14 *angel* evil angel. *still* always.   18 *better part of man* courage,
the quality which makes a man   20 *palter* deal deceitfully.   21–2 *keep . . .
hope* fulfill their promise in words but not in the sense we expect [K].   24 *gaze*
spectacle. *time* the times.   26 *Painted upon a pole* your picture painted on

And thou oppos'd, being of no woman born,
Yet I will try the last. Before my body
I throw my warlike shield. Lay on, Macduff,
And damn'd be him that first cries "Hold, enough!"

Exeunt fighting. Alarums.

*Retreat and flourish. Enter with
Drum and Colours, Malcolm, Siward,
Ross, Thanes, and Soldiers.*

MAL.   I would the friends we miss were safe arriv'd.   35

SIW.   Some must go off; and yet, by these I see,
So great a day as this is cheaply bought.

MAL.   Macduff is missing, and your noble son.

ROSS.   Your son, my lord, has paid a soldier's debt.
He only liv'd but till he was a man,   40
The which no sooner had his prowess confirm'd
In the unshrinking station where he fought
But like a man he died.

SIW.   Then he is dead?

ROSS.   Ay, and brought off the field. Your cause of sorrow
Must not be measur'd by his worth, for then   45
It hath no end.

SIW.   Had he his hurts before?

ROSS.   Ay, on the front.

SIW.   Why then, God's soldier be he!
Had I as many sons as I have hairs,
I would not wish them to a fairer death.
And so his knell is knoll'd.

MAL.   He's worth more sorrow,   50

canvas and set up in front of a showman's booth [K].   29 *baited* beset from all
sides (like a bear in bear-baiting).   32 *the last* the strength and valour, which
may yet prove stronger than fate [K].   33 *Lay on* strike hard.   36 *go off* die.
by judging by.   39 *paid a soldier's debt* since every soldier pledges his life to the
cause for which he fights [K].   42 *unshrinking station* (a) position from which he
did not retreat (b) status of manhood from which he did not shrink.   50 *knoll'd*
tolled.

And that I'll spend for him.

SIW.   He's worth no more.
They say he parted well and paid his score,
And so, God be with him! Here comes newer comfort.

Enter Macduff, *with* Macbeth's *head.*

MACD.   Hail, King! for so thou art. Behold where stands
Th' usurper's cursed head. The time is free.   55
I see thee compass'd with thy kingdom's pearl,
That speak my salutation in their minds;
Whose voices I desire aloud with mine —
Hail, King of Scotland!

ALL.   Hail, King of Scotland!   *Flourish.*

MAL.   We shall not spend a large expense of time   60
Before we reckon with your several loves
And make us even with you. My Thanes and kinsmen,
Henceforth be Earls, the first that ever Scotland
In such an honour nam'd. What's more to do
Which would be planted newly with the time —   65
As calling home our exil'd friends abroad
That fled the snares of watchful tyranny,
Producing forth the cruel ministers
Of this dead butcher and his fiendlike queen,
Who (as 'tis thought) by self and violent hands   70
Took off her life — this, and what needful else
That calls upon us, by the grace of Grace

---

55 *The time is free* the people of our time have been liberated (from the tyranny
of Macbeth).   56 *compass'd* surrounded.   60–75 *We shall . . . at Scone* The
method of Elizabethan tragedy required that the closing speech should be
uttered by the person of highest rank who survived, and this was seldom one of
the characters in whom we have taken most interest. Such speeches, therefore, are
always rather formal and serve as a kind of epilogue [K].   61 *reckon . . . loves*

We will perform in measure, time, and place.
So thanks to all at once and to each one,
Whom we invite to see us crown'd at Scone.

Flourish. Exeunt omnes.

---

reward the devotion that each of you has shown in my cause [K]. 65 *Which would . . . time* which the better times that have begun require to be established anew [K]. 68 *ministers* agents. 72 *calls upon us* demands my attention as King. 73 *in measure* with propriety and decorum, as opposed to the frantic rule of Macbeth [K].